Relativism

Relativism

Feet Firmly Planted in Mid-Air

Francis J. Beckwith and Gregory Koukl

BakerBooks
A Division of Baker Book House Co
Grand Rapids, Michigan 49516

Published by Baker Books
a division of Baker Book House Company
P.O. Box 6287, Grand Rapids, MI 49516-6287

Fifth printing, August 2001

Printed in the United States of America

Library of Congress Cataloging-in-Publication Data

Beckwith, Francis.
Relativism : feet firmly planted in mid-air / Francis J. Beckwith and Gregory Koukl.
p. cm.
Includes bibliographical references and index.
ISBN 0-8010-5806-6 (pbk.)
1. Ethical relativism—Controversial literature. I. Koukl, Gregory, 1950– . II. Title.
BJ1311.B39 1998
171'.7—dc21 98-17425

For current information about all releases from Baker Book House, visit our web site:
http://www.bakerbooks.com

To W. Howard Hoffman, M.D. Your generosity, encouragement, and friendship continue to be a testimony to your commitment to what is true, good, and beautiful. It is a privilege and a blessing to be a recipient of your personal and professional virtue.

—Francis J. Beckwith

To my brother Mark, who started me on this journey, and to my brother Dave, who began the adventure with me.

—Gregory Koukl

Contents

Acknowledgments 9
Introduction: Who Are You to Judge? 11

Part 1: Understanding Relativism
1. The Death of Truth 19
2. What Is Moral Relativism? 26
3. Three Kinds of Relativism 36

Part 2: Critiquing Relativism
4. Culture as Morality 43
5. Culture Defining Morality 49
6. Moral Common Sense 54
7. Relativism's Seven Fatal Flaws 61

Part 3: Relativism and Education
8. Values Clarification 73
9. Relativism's Offspring: Political Correctness and Multiculturalism 79
10. On the Road to Barbarism 92

Part 4: Relativism and Public Policy
11. Relativism and the Law 107
12. Relativism and the Meaning of Marriage 118
13. Relativism and the Meaning of Life 129

Part 5: Responding to Relativism
14. Tactics to Refute Relativism 143
15. Monkey Morality 156
16. Why Morality? 165

Notes 171
Index 182

Acknowledgments

A number of people deserve special acknowledgment for the parts they played in influencing and shaping my contribution to this book. First and foremost, my wife, Frankie, for her encouragement, support, love, and direction, whose presence never ceases to remind me that I may know a thing or two about the universe as a whole, but it is the particular things in it with which I have difficulty. A warm thank you to my students at Trinity International University, and those whom I had the privilege to teach at Whittier College (1996–97) and UNLV (1987–96), whose questions and insights, and intellectual prodding, have forced me to sharpen some of the arguments in this text. Amy Boucher Pye's editorial work and suggestions helped make my chapters accessible to a much wider audience.

Finally, I wish to thank some contemporary scholars who have had a strong influence on my intellectual development as well as the type of argument I present in this book: J. P. Moreland, Phillip Johnson, Hadley Arkes, John Warwick Montgomery, Michael Bauman, Francis Canavan, and Robert P. George. Any stature I may attain is the result of the shoulders on which I sit.

—Francis J. Beckwith

I'm indebted to a handful of people whose assistance was vital in the development of my thinking and the writing of this book. The late Dr. Francis Schaeffer provided a foundation for my thinking, and the very alive J. P. Moreland continues to build elegantly on that foundation, along with my other mentors in the philosophy department at Talbot School of Theology.

I received valuable editing help from Amy Boucher Pye at Baker, from Susan Titus-Osborne of Christian Communicators, and from Nancy Ulrich of Stand to Reason. I am also deeply indebted to the hard workers at Stand to Reason—especially Melinda Penner—for their continuous insight, encouragement, vision, and challenge.

Finally, I want to thank the thousands of people who over the years have called me during my radio program and given me a piece of their mind.

—Gregory Koukl

Introduction

Who Are You to Judge?

In America today we seem to think nothing of keeping *The Book of Virtues* and *The Bridges of Madison County* together on our coffee tables. And in these United States we say we firmly believe that truth and morality are relative while simultaneously decrying the absence of virtue and the rise of incivility.

We believe, or say we believe, that all people have a right to their own opinion—except those who hold that some opinions are better than others (though we believe that our opinion about them is better than their opinion about us). Our academic culture holds to the tenets of moral relativism while marginalizing those who apparently violate its rules against insensitivity, intolerance, and political incorrectness. We want to have our cake and eat it too.

And yet, despite this cultural equivalent of a multiple personality disorder, our headlines are filled with ethical, moral, and social issues, from abortion to physician-assisted suicide to affirmative action. Unfortunately, many today seem to assume that rational discussion has no place in the conflicts over moral questions and that no answers to such questions exist. Many believe that we are simply stuck with our opinions and that all opinions are relative—having no basis in any objective or unchanging moral truths.

Sex, Laws, and Videotapes

In the fall of 1992, I (Francis Beckwith) took part in a panel discussion on morality in the media. Sponsored by the Clark County Bar Association of Southern Nevada, the panel's purpose was to discuss the media's responsibility for the broadcasting of programs that contain sex, violence, and obscenity. Among the participants were two radio shock jocks, two attorneys (one of whom was a strong feminist), the owner of a phone sex line, the general manager of a local television station, a mother who schools her children at home, a Christian radio disc jockey, a television reporter, and me, a philosopher.

I agreed with most of the participants that government censorship is not the answer to our problems with the media. But I also made the point that a lack of censorship should not prevent the media from making moral judgments about their programming or from being concerned about how such programming may affect young people and the general populace negatively.

Immediately following these comments, a distressed young woman in the audience raised her hand and asked me the pointed question, "Who are you to judge?" This question, of course, was not meant to be answered. It was not an inquiry from someone seeking after truth but rather was a rhetorical question. For the young lady was really saying: Dr. Beckwith, you have no right to make moral judgments about individuals or society.

Though the question was not intended to be answered, I responded anyway: "I certainly do have a right to make moral judgments. I am a rational human person who is aware of certain fundamental principles of logical and moral reasoning. I think I'm qualified." This response absolutely shocked her. I continued, "Your claim that I have no right to make judgments is itself a judgment about me. Your claim, therefore, is self-refuting."

Although the audience was brought to laughter by this exchange, the young woman's question is a serious one raised by many people in our contemporary culture. It is serious because it assumes *moral relativism,* the view that when it comes to moral issues there are no universally objective right or wrong answers, no inappropriate or appropriate judgments, and no reasonable or rational ways by which to make moral distinctions that apply in every time, in every place, and to every person. Some people who espouse moral relativism seem to be saying that only subjective opinions exist, which are no different from one's feelings about a favorite football team, movie star, or ice cream flavor.

But the young woman in the audience did not fully comprehend the scope of her espousal of moral relativism. Although it is quite appealing in a culture whose elites instruct us to be "tolerant," "open-minded," and "nonjudgmental" (even though, ironically, such values are *inconsistent* with moral relativism), people who embrace this view rarely take it to its logical conclusion.

For to deny the existence of universally objective moral distinctions, one must admit that Mother Teresa was no more or less moral than Adolf Hitler, that torturing three-year-olds for fun is neither good nor evil, that giving 10 percent of one's financial surplus to an invalid is neither praiseworthy nor condemnable, that raping a woman is neither right nor wrong, and that providing food and shelter for one's spouse and children is neither a good thing nor a bad thing.

A Joint Response

It is in this climate of contradiction, inconsistency, and even coercion that Gregory Koukl and I address moral relativism, the unofficial creed of much of American culture, especially in the areas of education, law, and public policy. We write not merely to critique, but to equip all those who seek the truth in an age of confusion.

Although there are other types of relativism,[1] we will deal only with moral relativism, except for a brief portion of chapter 9 where we assess the views of those who argue that morality is relative *because* no knowledge, including moral knowledge, is objective.

It is evident that relativism has infested our society, affecting nearly every aspect of our public culture. The purpose of this book is to confront the challenge of relativism in a way that is not only intellectually rigorous but accessible to ordinary people who will be confronted by relativism in a number of different places, including their child's school curriculum, workplace conversations, the college classroom, the public square, and the church.

For all the complaints that conservatives have raised against relativism, there has been precious little published that can help people in their daily lives, including in the university classroom. This book is an attempt to meet their need.

Our Way Forward

Although this book is a joint effort, each author's primary responsibility should be acknowledged. Gregory Koukl is the author of chapters 1 through 7 and 14 through 16; Francis (Frank) Beckwith is the author of the introduction and chapters 9 through 13. Gregory and Frank coauthored chapter 8, and both critiqued, edited, and evaluated each other's work. At some points each incorporated the other's suggestions.

To avoid confusion, each author will speak in the first person plural throughout his chapter except when conveying his personal experience or something that cannot be adequately expressed in the first person plural. In those cases, he will speak in the first person singular.

In part 1 (chaps. 1–3), Gregory defines moral relativism and examines the three main varieties people encounter. He also explores the cultural setting in which relativism has become prevalent.

In chapters 4 through 7 (part 2), he sets forth a critique of this new philosophy and a defense of moral objectivism—the belief that objective moral standards exist that apply in every place, in every time, to every person.

In parts 3 and 4 Frank explains how moral relativism has influenced our public philosophy and how we approach social issues. Education is the focus of chapters 8 through 10. Chapter 8 (coauthored with Gregory) deals with the issue of values clarification and its impact on moral education. In chapters 9 and 10, Frank addresses the controversial topics of political correctness and multiculturalism, which presuppose moral relativism and deny objective truth.

How the concepts of personal autonomy and moral relativism have influenced our law and public culture are discussed in chapter 11. Chapters 12 and 13 explore the impact of relativism on three social issues: same-sex marriage, physician-assisted suicide, and abortion.

The book concludes with part 5, in which Gregory outlines responses to relativism. Chapter 14 gives tactics for refuting this philosophy.

Although one can certainly be a moral objectivist and not believe in God, in chapters 15 and 16 Gregory argues that a theistic universe—a universe in which God exists—best accounts for the existence of objective morality.

Part 1

Understanding Relativism

1

The Death of Truth

Allan Bloom, author of the landmark critique of American education *The Closing of the American Mind,* starts his analysis this way: "There is one thing a professor can be absolutely certain of: almost every student entering the university believes, or says he believes, that truth is relative. If this belief is put to the test, one can count on the students' reaction: they will be uncomprehending. That anyone should regard the proposition as not self-evident astonishes them, as though he were calling into question 2 + 2 = 4."[1]

What Professor Bloom observes is not a trend but a revolution. Like most revolutions, it did not start with a rifle shot or a cannon but with an idea that was whispered in many different environments and diverse situations. This revolution started in academia and eventually engulfed the common person. Its growth has been so subtle and thorough that it is now a core belief—not just of the college elite, but also of the rank and file, white collar and blue collar alike.

What Is Truth?

Since the sixties we have been in the throes of this quiet but desperate revolution of thought—the death of truth. We don't mean "truth" in the sense of something being my personal opinion. Rather we refer to the death of what the late Dr. Francis Schaeffer called "true truth," the extinction of the idea that any particular thing can be known for sure.

Today we've lost the confidence that statements of fact can ever be anything more than just opinions; we no longer know that anything is certain beyond our subjective preferences. The word *truth* now means "true for me" and nothing more. We have entered an era of dogmatic skepticism.

Ideas that are whispered are seldom analyzed well, for they simply don't draw enough attention. By means of repetition and passive acceptance over time, they take on the force of common wisdom, a "truth" that everyone knows but no one has stopped to examine, a kind of intellectual urban legend.

Once ideas like these take root, they are difficult to dislodge. Attempts to do so result in Bloom's "uncomprehending" stares.[2] The ideas become so much a part of our emerging intellectual constitution that we are increasingly incapable of critical self-reflection. Even if we did, we have little conviction that such analysis would do any good anyway. As Kelly Monroe remarked in her book *Finding God at Harvard,* "Students feel safer as doubters than as believers, and as perpetual seekers rather than eventual finders."[3]

When truth dies, all of its subspecies, such as ethics, perish with it. If truth can't be known, then the concept of moral truth becomes incoherent. Ethics become relative, right and wrong matters of individual opinion. This may seem a moral liberty, but it ultimately rings hollow. "The freedom of our day," lamented a graduate in a Harvard commencement address, "is the freedom to devote ourselves to any values we please, on the mere condition that we do not believe them to be true."[4]

The death of truth in our society has created a moral decay in which "every debate ends with the barroom question 'says who?'"[5] When we abandon the idea that one set of laws applies to every human being, all that remains is subjective, personal opinion.

Pleasure as Ethics

When morality is reduced to personal tastes, people exchange the moral question, What *is* good? for the pleasure question, What *feels* good? They assert their desires and then attempt to rationalize their choices with moral language. In this case, the tail wags the dog. Instead of morality constraining pleasures ("I want to do that, but I really shouldn't"), the pleasures define morality ("I want to do that, and I'm going to find a way to rationalize it"). This effort at ethical decision making is really nothing more than thinly veiled self-interest—pleasure as ethics.

When self-interest rules, it has a profound impact on behavior, especially affecting how we treat other human beings. The notions of human respect and dignity depend on the existence of moral truth. Without it, there is no obligation of self-sacrifice on behalf of others. Instead, we can discard people when they become troublesome or expensive, or simply when they cramp our lifestyles.

What follows is a true story about a newborn child we'll call Baby Garcia. This event took place in a major hospital in the Los Angeles area. I pass on the exact details as Jennifer, the nurse involved, related them to me:

> One night a nurse on my shift came up to me and said, "Jennifer, you need to see the Garcia baby." There was something suspicious about the way she said it, though. *I see babies born every hour*, I thought.
>
> She led me to a utility room the nurses used for their breaks. Women were smoking and drinking coffee, their feet up on the stainless steel counter. There, lying on the metal, was the naked body of a newborn baby.
>
> "What is this baby doing here on this counter?" I asked timidly.
>
> "That's a preemie born at nineteen weeks," she said. "We don't do anything to save them unless they're twenty weeks."
>
> I noticed that his chest was fluttering rapidly. I picked him up for a closer look. "This baby is still alive!" I exclaimed. I thought they hadn't noticed.
>
> Then I learned the horrible truth. The nurses knew, and it didn't matter. They had presented the baby to its mother as a dead, premature child. Then they took him away and tossed him on the cold, steel counter in the lunch room until he died. His skin was blotchy white, and his mouth was gaping open as he tried to breathe.
>
> I did the one thing I could think of. I held him in his last moments so he'd at least have some warmth and love when he died.

Just then one of the nurses—a large, harsh woman—burst into the room. "Jennifer, what are you doing with that baby?" she yelled.

"He's still alive . . ."

"He's still alive because you're holding him," she said. Grabbing him by the back with one hand, she snatched him from me, opened one of the stainless steel cabinets, and pulled out a specimen container with formaldehyde in it. She tossed the baby in and snapped the lid on. It was over in an instant.

To them, this child wasn't human. In seven more days he would have qualified, but at nineteen weeks he was just trash. [6]

If there is no truth, nothing has transcendent value, including human beings. The death of morality reduces people to the status of mere creatures. When persons are viewed as things, they begin to be treated as things.

Anything Goes

The death of morality also produces an "anything goes" mentality. Sexual norms not only become more liberal, they expand without boundaries because no boundaries exist. Ann Landers recorded the following letter from one of her "morally liberated" readers:

Dear Ann:

I am a man in my early 60s, divorced and retired. My sister is in her late 50s and widowed. We go to bed together twice a week. This has been going on since her husband died 8 years ago. Actually, when we were teenagers, we fooled around a lot, but never had intercourse. This is not a love match, but it is sex, and good sex at that.

We both enjoy these escapades, and they always produce a good night's sleep. No one knows about this, and no one is getting hurt, or do you think we are fooling ourselves?

—No NAME, NO CITY, PLEASE

Dear No Name:

Sick, sick, sick. If I had your address I would send you a "get well" card.[7]

Even more sobering is how America responded when art went on trial in a Cincinnati courthouse. At issue was an exhibit in the Contemporary Art Center of the work of Robert Mapplethorpe, a talented photographer who had distinguished himself with, among other things, still-life photography of flowers. The photographs on display included the following: a picture of a ten-year-old girl sitting in a chair with her knees up and genitals exposed; a photograph of a man who was naked except for cowboy boots, bent over with a bull-whip in his anus; and a shot of one man expelling a stream of urine into the mouth of another.

The museum was charged with exhibiting pornography. During the trial, a curator of another museum who testified on behalf of the Mapplethorpe exhibit was asked if the urination picture was art.

"Yes," she said.

"Is it fine art?"

"Yes."

"Why?"

"Because of the composition and the lighting."

Each photograph was acquitted of the charge of pornography and judged as fine art, after which social commentator and radio talk-show host Dennis Prager observed, "Ladies and gentlemen, if some of the leading artists in a civilization see a man urinating in another man's mouth and see composition and lighting and do not see their civilization being pissed upon, we are in trouble."[8]

And we are in trouble. A security camera in Britain records two young boys calmly leading a toddler away and later bludgeoning him to death. A mother in South Carolina fastens her own two children snugly into their safety belts and then sinks the car in the river so she can restore a romantic interest with a man who doesn't want her kids.[9] The leader of a national animal rights organization states that animals are the moral equivalent of humans.[10] An upper-middle-class college couple in New Jersey deliver a child in a motel room, bash in its head, and then drop it in a dumpster. The American College of Emergency Physicians estimates that seventy thousand elderly Americans were abandoned by family members in one year, a practice called "granny dumping."[11] And the list goes on.

We are not trying to pander to the sensational with these illustrations. These events aren't out of the ordinary; they can be seen almost daily in our living rooms on the evening news.

Ours is a generation that has institutionalized moral relativism. We've cut our eye-teeth on the philosophy that life's most sublime goal is to be happy and that virtually any means justifies this self-serving end. No longer will we allow a hint of moral censure on sexual practices that were regarded as perverse only a generation before. We consider bullwhips in the butt and urination in the face fine art, abortion a constitutional right, infanticide a reasonable alternative to caring for a child with a troublesome birth defect, lesbian and homosexual families normal, and drug use a national pastime.

"It is possible," Prager observes, "that some societies have declined as rapidly as has America since the 1960s, but I am not aware of any."[12]

Traitors in Our Midst

This is not a "morality" we simply tolerate; we champion it. We take pride in our tolerance, yet tolerate no one who doesn't share our moral open-mindedness. "Who are you to pass judgment?" we ask. "Where do you get off condemning a nurse for what she does with a fetus that was dying anyway? Or for criticizing the sexual preferences of siblings? Or for challenging another's view of art?"

This stinking stew of ethical nothingness is the sad legacy of the sixties. Yet when our own moral philosophy turns us into victims—when our personal liberty is interrupted by random acts of anarchy—suddenly something like moral consciousness tries to lift its head.

Take the Los Angeles riots of 1992, for example. As the buildings burned we watched with horror. Shops were plundered not by hooded looters but by families made up of mom, dad, and the kids—moral mutants on the shopping spree of their lives, giggling and laughing with impunity while stuffing their spoils into shopping carts and oversized trash bags.

We shouldn't have been surprised. During the L.A. riots these families did exactly what they had been taught. Nobody wanted to "impose" their morality on anyone else, so they learned that values are relative and that morality is a matter of personal preference. Make your own rules, define your own reality, seek your own truth.

In the spring of '92, thousands of people did just what we told them to do, and civilization burned.

If we reject truth, why should we be surprised at the moral turbulence that follows? As C. S. Lewis said, "We laugh at honor and are shocked to find traitors in our midst. We castrate and bid the geldings be fruitful."[13]

This is the chaotic and confusing world of moral relativism, a world made more confusing because moral relativism isn't even moral. It doesn't qualify as a genuine moral view, as we will learn in the next chapter.

2

What Is Moral Relativism?

Before defining moral relativism, we need to make two distinctions. The first regards what we mean when we say something is right or wrong, and the second deals with the difference between a subjective and an objective truth.

Two Wrongs, Two Rights

The statements "One ought not kill innocent people" and "One ought to believe that Kansas is in the United States" are two entirely different kinds of statements. Both make truth claims, but they differ in that each distinguishes a kind of "ought"—one the moral ought and the other the rational ought. The first suggests a moral obligation; the second an obligation based on reason.

There are two kinds of oughts, and there are two ways to be wrong about something. We can be wrong by being irrational, or we can be wrong by being unethical. Morality deals with the second.

Rational errors can be distinguished from moral wrongs in this way. Nineteenth-century philosopher John Stuart Mill pointed out that moral wrongs are the kinds of things for which punishment seems justified.[1] We don't punish people merely for getting their sums wrong in math. Their errors would be rational, not moral. But a man who beats his wife is not simply incorrect; he's immoral. When there is a rational wrong, we correct the error. When there is a moral wrong, we correct—or punish—the person.

Two Truths

Just as there are two ways to be right or wrong, there are also two ways for something to be true: it can be subjectively true or it can be objectively true.

When I say, "Häagen-Dazs butter pecan ice cream is absolutely delicious," I have said something true, because this statement accurately reflects my personal tastes.[2] Notice, however, that what I have said is not really about ice cream. I have not made a claim about an object outside of me, a half-eaten pint of frozen dessert sitting on my counter. Rather I have said something about the subject, me.

My statement about the taste of Häagen-Dazs ice cream is a *subjective* truth. It is true for me, the subject, but not for the object, the ice cream itself. The ice cream doesn't "taste"; I taste it. The experience of flavor pertains to me as a subject, not to the ice cream as an object. That's why when I comment on the flavor, I'm talking about something true about me, not about the ice cream—subjective, not objective.

Tastes are personal. They're private. They're individual. If you didn't like butter pecan and favored chocolate instead, it would be strange to say that you were wrong. You should not be faulted, it seems, for having different subjective tastes about desserts than someone else.

What if my claim was not about flavors, though, but about numbers? If I say that the sum of two plus two is four, I'm making a different sort of claim than stating my taste in ice cream. As a subject, I'm communicating a belief that I hold about an external, *objective* truth.

If you disagreed and said that two plus two equals five, I could claim you were wrong without being accused of an impropriety. In themselves, mathematical equations are either true or false, having one right answer. They do not have a variety of "right" answers that vary according to individual tastes. If we disagreed on the sum, we'd adjudicate between our two opinions by examining the object itself. Our goal would not be to share our feelings but to find the correct answer, because in this case we believe the truth to be objective or "out there," not subjective or "in here."

Subjective truths are based on internal preferences and change according to our whims. Objective truths, in contrast, are realities in the external world that we discover and cannot be changed by our internal feelings. External facts are what they are, regardless of how we feel about them.

Doing Their Own Thing

Building on our definitions of objective and subjective truth, we can now see that moral relativism is a type of subjectivism. It holds that moral truths are preferences much like our taste in ice cream. The validity of these truths depends entirely on the one who says, "It's true *for me* [the subject] if I believe it."

Moral relativism teaches that when it comes to morals, that which is ethically right or wrong, people do their own thing. Ethical truths depend on the individuals and groups who hold them.

Believing that ethical truth is subjective, moral relativists therefore react to moral judgments about sexual behavior, for example, much as if someone said they were wrong because of their choice of desserts: "Who are you to tell me what I ought to prefer?" To them the words *ought* and *should* are meaningless because everyone's morality is equal; no one has a claim to a morality that is incumbent on others.

Relativism does not require a particular behavior for everyone in similar moral situations. When faced with exactly the same ethical situation, I might choose one thing, but you may choose the opposite. No universal rules apply to everyone.[3]

Moral relativism is contrasted with moral absolutism, which can mean different things. Minimally, moral absolutism holds that a moral rule is true regardless of whether anyone believes it. It can't be created by personal conviction; nor does it disappear when an individual or culture rejects it. Even if ignored, objective moral rules still maintain their ethical force and are universally binding in all similar cases.[4]

Absolutists hold that moral rules are frequently self-evident in the same way that mathematical truth is self-evident. We don't invent morality; we discover it like we discover multiplication tables.

Revising the Standard

Relativism as a moral system is revisionist because it seeks to redefine what it means to be moral, measuring it by a new standard.

Classically, moral systems have had at least three characteristics.[5] First, morality has been viewed as a supremely authoritative guide to action, trumping considerations of preference, taste, custom, self-interest, or individual fancy. Moral questions are among the most important we can ask, holding the highest priority in life.

Second, morality includes a prescriptive code of conduct. It doesn't merely *describe* a state of affairs; it *directs* how things should be. Moral rules are action guides that carry with them a sense of obligation, defining how people *ought* to conduct themselves. These injunctions apply not just to actions but to attitudes and motives as well.

Third, morality is universal. Moral rules are not arbitrary and personal but are public, applying equally to all people in relevantly similar situations. If a specific act is wrong for one person, then it is equally wrong for another.

Eighteenth-century Scottish philosopher David Hume describes the universal nature of morality this way: "The notion of morals implies some sentiment common to all mankind which recommends the same object to general approbation and makes every man or most men agree in the same opinion or same discussion concerning it. It also implies some sentiments so universal and comprehensive as to extend to all mankind."[6]

These last two characteristics—the "oughtness" of morality and the universal nature of moral rules—are important criteria. Relativism, however, rejects all universal moral rules and abandons the idea of oughtness. It does not refine our understanding of what morality entails but rather rejects it.

Indeed, relativism does not even qualify as an ethical system. We can prove this a couple of ways.

No Real Difference

What's the difference between a relativist and a person who admits she has no morality at all? There seems to be none.

How does a relativist make a moral decision? He decides for himself whatever he thinks is best. How does someone with no morality know how to act? She decides for herself whatever she thinks is best.

Even those people with no scruples whatsoever can be said to have "their own" morality. This illustrates the problem precisely. How can we make sense of an alleged morality that functions the same as not having any morality at all? If a thing cannot be distinguished from its opposite, then the distinction between the two is meaningless.

Thus the first reason relativism does not qualify as an ethical viewpoint is that the "morality" of relativism is no different than having no morality at all.

Relativism's Moral Hero

Another way to assess the validity of a moral system is to see what kind of person it produces. Given a particular standard of morality, the person who is most moral is the one who practices the specific system's key moral rule consistently.

To assess the value of the moral rule, Love your neighbor as yourself, for example, look at the principle in action. When this ethic is practiced consistently, it produces someone like Mother Teresa, who was thoroughly selfless and always gave to others. The moral system is validated by the kind of moral hero that results.

The consistent practice of the morality of nonviolent passive resistance results in a Mahatma Gandhi. The moral principle requiring perfect obedience to the Father in heaven found its most sublime expression in Jesus of Nazareth. In each case, the quality of the moral hero—the one who most closely lives the ideal—indicates the quality of the moral system.

What kind of moral champion does relativism produce? What is the best that relativism has to offer? What do we call those who most thoroughly apply the principles of relativism, caring nothing for others' ideas of right or wrong, those who are unmoved by others' notions of ethical standards and instead consistently follow the beat of their own moral drum?

In our society, we have a name for these people; they are a homicide detective's worst nightmare. The quintessential relativist is a sociopath, one with no conscience. This is what relativism produces.

Something is terribly wrong with an alleged moral point of view that produces a sociopath as its brightest star. This is another reason relativism does not qualify as an ethical viewpoint.

Relativism does not stand in any great moral tradition. Rather, it has been universally rejected by all. The supreme moral teachers of all time—Moses, Jesus, the apostle Paul, Buddha, Aristotle, Gandhi, Martin Luther King Jr.—have all condemned this view.

Relativism simply is not a moral point of view. Its "morality" is no different than having no morality at all, its moral hero is a sociopath, and it has been opposed by every moral tradition. Those who are relativists have no morality.

Some people will object to this characterization because they wish to keep the label "moral," regardless of their ethics. "How dare you say I have no morality!" they protest. "I have a morality. I do whatever I please. That's my morality."

That's our point. Those who are relativists do whatever they want, and doing whatever one wants is not morality. Morality is doing what's right, not necessarily what's pleasant.

The Myth of Moral Neutrality

One of the most entrenched assumptions of relativism is that there is such a thing as morally neutral ground, a place of complete impartiality where no judgments or any "forcing" of personal views are allowed. Each person takes a neutral posture toward the moral conviction of others. This is the essence of tolerance, the argument goes.

Moral neutrality, though, is a myth, as the next illustration shows. Faye Wattleton, the former president of Planned Parenthood, wrote the following piece, "Self-Definition: Morality."

> Like most parents, I think that a sense of moral responsibility is one of the greatest gifts I can give my child. But teaching morality doesn't mean imposing *my* moral value on others. It means sharing wisdom, giving reasons for believing as I do—and then trusting others to think and judge for *themselves.*
>
> My parents' morals were deeply rooted in religious conviction but tempered by tolerance—the essence of which is respect for other people's views. They taught me that reasonable people may differ on moral issues, and that fundamental respect for others is morality of the highest order.
>
> I have devoted my career to ensuring a world in which my daughter, Felicia, can inherit that legacy. I hope the tolerance and respect I show her as a parent is reinforced by the work she sees me doing every day: fighting for the right of all individuals to make their own moral decisions about childbearing.
>
> Seventy-five years ago, Margaret Sanger founded Planned Parenthood to liberate individuals from the "mighty engines of repression." As she wrote, "The men and women of America are demanding that . . . they be allowed to mold their lives, not at the arbitrary command of church or state but as their conscience and judgment may dictate."
>
> I'm proud to continue that struggle, to defend the rights of all people to their own beliefs. When others try to inflict their views on me, my daughter or anyone else, that's not morality: It's tyranny. It's unfair, and it's un-American.[7]

This is impressively and persuasively written, one of the finest expressions of this view available in the space of five short paragraphs. It sounds so sensible, so reasonable, and so tolerant, but there's a fundamental flaw.

Wattleton's assessment is based on the notion of neutral ground, a place where one can stand that implies no moral judgment. Wattleton is not neutral, however, as her own comments demonstrate.

In her article, Wattleton in effect argues that each of us *should* respect another's point of view. She then implies, however, that any point of view other than this one is immoral, un-American, and tyrannous. If you disagree with Wattleton's position that all points of view are equally valid, then your point of view is not valid. Her argument self-destructs.

In fact, Wattleton seeks to impose her own absolute on other people: "Fundamental respect for others is morality of the highest order." This is a personal moral position she strives to mandate politically. She writes, "I have devoted my career to ensuring a world in which my daughter, Felicia, can inherit that legacy." What legacy? Her point of view. How does she ensure this? By passing laws. Wattleton has devoted her career to ensuring a world in which her point of view is enforced by law.

We don't object to the political process being used to enforce a particular point of view. What is so disturbing in Wattleton's article is her implication that she is neutral, unbiased, and tolerant, when she is not. The only place of true neutrality is silence. Speak up, give your opinion, state your view, and you forfeit your claim to neutrality.

As a case in point, in May, 1994, Congress passed a law making it a federal offense to block an abortion clinic.[8] Pamela Maraldo, then president of Planned Parenthood, commented to the press, "This law goes to show that no one can force their viewpoint on someone else." But the self-contradiction of her statement is obvious. All laws force someone's viewpoint.

Moral neutrality seems virtuous, but there's no benefit, only danger. In our culture we don't stop at "sharing wisdom, giving reasons for believing as [we] do—and then trusting others to think and judge for themselves," nor should we. This leads to anarchy. Instead we use moral reasoning, public advocacy, and legislation to encourage virtue and discourage dangerous and morally inappropriate behavior. That is, if we haven't been struck morally paralyzed by relativism.

Our Moral Illiteracy

Relativism today has produced a profound moral illiteracy. Kelly Monroe, editor of *Finding God at Harvard,* calls it "American roulette—'Just Say No' and 'Just Do It' without recognition of a moral reality to decide which to do when."[9] A society held captive by relativism begins to lose its capacity to think in morally coherent ways or even to draw the most obvious ethical conclusions.

A perfect example of this comes from a conversation I had with an assistant in a doctor's office. While she prepped me for an examination, I decided to get her opinion about the nature of morality.

"Can I ask you a personal question?" I asked. She paused in her work, uncertain how to respond. "I'm reading a book on ethics, and I want to know your opinion about something."

"Oh," she said. "Okay."

"Do you believe that morality is absolute, or do all people decide for themselves?"

"What do you mean by morality?" she asked.

"Simply put, what's right and what's wrong," I answered.

We talked back and forth for a few minutes, and it became evident to me that she was having a difficult time even comprehending the questions I was asking about moral categories. I thought maybe a clear-case example would make the task simpler, a question with an obvious answer, such as, Who is buried in Grant's tomb? or, How long was the Hundred Years War?

"Is murder wrong?" I asked. "Is it wrong to take an innocent human life?"

She waffled. "Well . . ."

"Well . . . what?"

"Well, I'm thinking."

I was surprised at her hesitation. "What I'm trying to find out is whether morals, right and wrong, are something we make up for ourselves or something we discover. In other words, do morals apply whether we believe in them or not?"

I waited. "Can we say that taking innocent life is morally acceptable?"

"I guess it depends," she said tentatively.

"Depends on what?" I asked.

"It depends on what other people think or decide."

I'll make this really easy, I thought. "Do you think torturing babies for fun is wrong?"

"Well . . . I wouldn't want them to do that to my baby."

"You've missed the point of my question," I said, a bit exasperated. "I may not like burned food, but that doesn't mean giving it to me is immoral. Do you believe there is any circumstance, in any culture, at any time in history, in which torturing babies just for pure pleasure could be justified? Is it objectively wrong, or is it just a matter of opinion?"

There was a long pause. Finally she answered, "People should all be allowed to decide for themselves."

In reflecting on this conversation, I realized that I would never want this woman on a jury. I would never want her as a social worker, as an employee of a bank, as a teacher, as any kind of medical practitioner, or in any branch of law enforcement. I would not want a person who thinks like this in any position of public trust.

Sadly, this woman's view of ethics is repeated time after time in every level of society. In reality, if she was awakened in the middle of the night by the plaintive screams of a young child being tormented by her neighbor next door, I'm sure she would be horrified by the barbarism. Her moral intuitions would immediately rise to the surface and she'd recoil at such evil. In a discussion of the issue, however, she seemed incapable of admitting that even this egregious wrong was actually immoral.

My conversation with the doctor's assistant shows how muddled a person's thinking can become after a steady diet of moral relativism.

3

Three Kinds of Relativism

Most people will encounter three main varieties of moral relativism. The first view is not strictly about morality but about culture, referring to anthropology and not ethics per se. The other two are bona fide subjectivist moral theses that differ in who defines moral boundaries. One holds that *society* at large is the subject that determines the relativistic standards. The other view sees the relevant moral decision-maker as the *individual.* One's personal preferences, not society's norms, guide moral judgments.

In this brief chapter we will give a thumbnail sketch of each of these views. Our fuller critique will follow in part 2.

Society Does Relativism

Many people try to justify moral relativism by making the observation that cultures seem to differ regarding basic moral values. Anthropologists record that apparently each society has different ethical standards when it comes to morals. This brand of ethics is what we call Society Does Relativism. It's also known as cultural or descriptive relativism.

For example, philosopher Tom Beauchamp describes certain conduct of seventeenth-century Hudson Bay tribes as completely "moral" to them but deeply offensive to the ethical sensibilities of European explorers: "Members of these tribes practiced a custom of killing their parents when they had become old and incapable of supporting themselves by their labor. Elderly parents were strangled by their children, who, natives believed, had an obligation to perform this ritual act. . . . Should a tribe member suffer the misfortune of having no children to perform this duty, the custom was to request the service from friends. . . . A refusal was viewed as a humiliation for the person making the request; dying for the sake of the group was a point of honor in these tribes."[1]

Proponents of Society Does Relativism take the differences in moral opinions between cultures as an argument for relativism over moral objectivism. Since each culture has a different morality, none is justified in claiming that its own brand of morality is correct. Therefore, there is no objective morality nor any moral absolutes. Morality is relative.

Society Says Relativism

The second type of relativism is different from the first in a very important way. Society Does Relativism is *descriptive* only, merely reporting on the way cultures appear to act. It is not *prescriptive* or normative because it makes no judgment on behavior and offers no guidelines for conduct. It does not tell how things ought to be.

The second type of relativism, however, goes beyond anthropology—mere cultural observations—into the area of genuine morality. In contrast to the first, it prescribes how one should act.

Society Says Relativism, also known as conventionalism or normative ethical relativism, teaches that all people ought to act in keeping with their own society's code. What is right for one society isn't necessarily right for another. People ought to do whatever their "society says" to do.

"Trekkers" will recognize Society Says Relativism because it is practiced by the crew of the Enterprise in *Star Trek*. The Prime Directive of the Federation is that all cultural values are equally valid, even though they may conflict with the preferences of the Federation.

Beauchamp distinguishes between two types of normative relativism: "This thesis is normative, because it makes a value judgment; it delineates which standards or norms legitimately determine right and wrong behavior. One form of this normative relativism asserts that one ought to do what one's own society or dominant group determines to be right—a *group* form of normative relativism—and a second form holds that one ought to do what one personally believes to be right—an *individual* form of normative relativism. Thus there are two distinct forms of normative relativism" (emphasis in the original).[2]

In Society Says Relativism, moral standards are set by one's culture. The third kind of relativism (Beauchamp's second form of normative relativism) is more radical.

I Say Relativism

In I Say Relativism, also known as individual ethical relativism or ethical subjectivism, individual preferences offer the only guidelines to behavior. What is right for one person isn't necessarily right for another person, regardless of the culture in which they live.

Each person acts as his conscience dictates, in keeping with his personal moral code. Though this code may change as time goes on and preferences vary, morality remains personal and subjective. I Say Relativism is often characterized by the response, Who are you to say how I ought to live?

A clarification needs to be made here. Even moral objectivists acknowledge that some ethical decisions are personal judgment calls about things that are, arguably, morally benign in themselves. Because these moral decisions offend the conscience of some, however, they abstain.

Even the Bible—a standard source of moral guidelines for ethical objectivists—teaches latitude in some areas. The apostle Paul says, "One person has faith that he may eat all things, but he who is weak eats vegetables only. . . . One person regards one day above another,

another regards every day alike." He then adds, "Each person must be fully convinced in his own mind."[3] Some issues are personal, the apostle argues, and are therefore matters of individual conscience.

In contrast, I Say Relativism is much more extreme. In ethical subjectivism, everything is a private judgment call. All morality is personal; none is public. Every moral evaluation is a mere opinion, a personal preference.

This is why relativists are so quick to say, "Don't force your morality on me," for no external code of conduct is legitimate in their view. Morality is private. The biblical description of this type of ethic is found in the Book of Judges where "Every man did what was right in his own eyes."[4]

Questions to Ponder

As we think about the various types of ethical relativism in the pages that follow, we will examine questions such as the following:

What kinds of things are moral rules?

Is morality a subjective thing like taste in ice cream, or is it an objective thing like mathematical equations?

Is it conventional, changing with our whims or our culture, or is it fixed and absolute?

Do we judge morality, or does morality judge us?

Part 2

Critiquing Relativism

4

Culture as Morality

In *Folkways,* a classic presentation of cultural or Society Does Relativism, anthropologist William Graham Sumner argues that all morality can be explained in naturalistic, cultural terms. Morality, he claims, is not objective in any sense. Instead it finds its genesis in the subjective conventions of culture, known as folkways and mores.

Sumner makes three observations to support his view. First, he observes that each culture has a unique set of moral values.

Second, he claims these moral values are generated by the natural influence of pain and pleasure as people seek to satisfy their base wants and desires. The values create a complex system of customs that reflect notions of decency, duty, propriety, rights, respect, reverence, and so on, and regulate culture for the general welfare. Laws are enacted as mechanical, utilitarian devices to enforce the most vital mores.

Third, Sumner argues that each group thinks its moral values are right and the others are wrong.

Sumner concludes that morality is conventional and that all so-called "moral instincts" are nothing more than cultural biases. "'Immoral' never means anything but contrary to the mores of the time and place,"[1] he states. "'Rights' are the rules of mutual give and take in the competition of life. . . . Therefore rights can never be 'natural' or 'God-given,' or absolute in any sense."[2]

We will make three observations in critique of this view.[3]

Don't Eat Grandma

Sumner's entire thesis hinges on his first claim, that each culture has a unique set of moral values. That societies do, in fact, differ much in their core moral convictions, however, is not obviously true.

At first glance, the wide variations in moral practices of various cultures seem to indicate a broad diversity of basic moral values. Conduct appropriate in one culture is loathed in another. Early Hudson Bay tribes thought patricide was noble. In India before the British came, Hindu widows in a practice called suttee threw themselves alive on the funeral pyre of their dead husbands. In European cultures, both practices are considered immoral.

A closer look, however, reveals another picture. Apparent moral differences often represent differences only in perception of the facts of a circumstance and not a conflict in the values themselves.

Facts are descriptive, answering the question, What *is* the case? A fetus is or isn't human. Euthanasia is or isn't an example of murder. Values, on the other hand, are prescriptive, answering the question, What *ought* to be the case? One ought not murder. Life ought to be more important than choice.

Unjustified killing of human beings (murder) has been wrong in every culture at every time in history; what has changed is the concept of justification. Hitler justified killing Jews because he considered them subhuman. In the Hudson Bay tribes, children strangled their own parents as an act of kindness instead of letting them live to what they saw as an unproductive old age. "Dying for the sake of the group was a point of honor in these tribes."[4] The underlying moral rule that it is noble to die for the welfare of many is one all cultures share. Indeed, that's what soldiers do.

Hindus value the universal virtues of chastity and purity in their women so much that grieving wives express this virtue through a culturally determined practice: self-immolation. The word *suttee* comes from the Sanskrit word *sati*, meaning "chaste and pure wife."

Another example is the dispute over abortion, which we will examine in more length in chapter 13. Much of the debate turns out to be a conflict about facts, not fundamental values. Those who are pro-life think abortion is wrong because it takes the life of an innocent human person without proper justification. In most cases, those favoring abortion agree that human persons are valuable. They disagree, though, on whether the unborn child is, in fact, an example of an innocent human person. Here the fundamental values are the same, but there is disagreement over the relevant facts that influence the application of the standard.

In India, cows roam free because Hindus consider them sacred. In America we eat beef. At first glance it would seem we have conflicting values, but both of our cultures hold that it is wrong to eat other human beings. In America when Grandma dies, we don't eat her, we bury her. In India, Hindus don't eat cattle because they believe the cow *may be* grandma reincarnated in another form.[5]

In each of these cases, the apparent moral differences arise not because of conflicting values but because of facts pertaining to common values. C. S. Lewis argues that a common foundation of morality underlies all human cultures. "If anyone will take the trouble to compare the moral teaching of, say, the ancient Egyptians, Babylonians, Hindus, Chinese, Greeks, and Romans, what will really strike him will be how very like they are to each other and to our own."[6] He lists these basic moral tenets in his book *The Abolition of Man.*

Genuine areas of value dispute are rare. To test for value differences, cite the foundational moral rule one culture affirms and the other denies. True moral conflicts are those that remain when all factual differences are eliminated.

Thus the first problem with Society Does Relativism is that its underlying assumption is false. In many cases, apparent moral discrepancies between cultures represent only a difference in the perception of the facts of a circumstance, not a conflict in the values themselves. But another difficulty is more subtle.

Anthropology versus Morality

Even if relativists are right that cultures differ radically in their basic moral values, so what? The observation itself proves nothing. Just because cultures differ on moral viewpoints doesn't mean objective moral truth is a fiction. In logic this is called a non sequitur; the conclusion doesn't follow from the premises.

Sumner is an anthropologist, so it is not surprising that he makes anthropological observations. But the problem is that observations about the differing values between groups of people, even if accurate (and we contend these aren't), don't translate into valid conclusions about the true nature of morality per se.

How does it follow that because each group thinks it is right, therefore no group is correct? The simple fact of disagreement on morality does not lead to the conclusion that there is no moral truth. This confuses the epistemological issue (the accurate *knowledge* of objective values) with the ontological issue (the *existence* of objective values).

Currently there are conflicting views on many things. Is homosexuality genetically determined, or is it developmental (or some combination of the two)? Are humans defined by their body, brain, and central nervous system, or do they also possess an immaterial soul? Is there life after death, or do we perish with our bodies? Does the disappearance of equatorial rain forests pose a threat to civilization? Is the protective ozone layer that covers the earth being destroyed?

Opinions on each of these issues vary. The fact that there is disagreement, however, does not mean that no view can be correct. The same is true with differences of opinion on morality.

As we can see from the second point, Society Does Relativism is not a moral thesis at all. The only thing one can safely conclude from anthropology is that people have different points of view about right and wrong. That's all. Nothing more.

The Problem with the Elephant

Sumner stumbles a third time when he states, "Every attempt to win an outside standpoint from which to reduce the whole to an absolute philosophy of truth and right, based on an unalterable principle, is delusion."[7]

Sumner is making a strong claim here about knowledge. He says that all claims to know objective moral truth are false because we are all imprisoned in our own culture and are incapable of seeing beyond the limits of our own biases. He concludes, therefore, that moral truth is relative to culture and that no objective standard exists.

Sumner's analysis falls victim to the same error committed by religious pluralists who see all religions as equally valid. They use the popular Eastern story of the blind men and the elephant to illustrate.

In the children's book *The Blind Men and the Elephant,* Lillian Quigley retells the ancient fable of six blind men who visit the palace of the Rajah and encounter an elephant for the first time. As each touches the elephant with his hands, he announces his discoveries.

> The first blind man put out his hand and touched the side of the elephant. "How smooth! An elephant is like a wall." The second blind man put out his hand and touched the trunk of the elephant. "How round! An elephant is like a snake." The third blind man put out his hand and touched the tusk of the elephant. "How sharp! An elephant is like a spear." The fourth blind man put out his hand and touched the leg of the elephant. "How tall! An elephant is like a tree." The fifth blind man reached out his hand and touched the ear of the elephant. "How wide! An elephant is like a fan." The sixth blind man put out his hand and touched the tail of the elephant. "How thin! An elephant is like a rope."[8]

An argument ensues as each blind man makes a claim for his own perception of the elephant. The Rajah, awakened by the commotion, calls out from the balcony, "The elephant is a big animal. Each man touched only one part. You must put all the parts together to find out what an elephant is like."

Enlightened by the Rajah's wisdom, the blind men reach agreement. "Each one of us knows only a part. To find out the whole truth we must put all the parts together."[9]

This fable is often used to illustrate one of two points. The religious application holds that each religious view is only part of a larger truth and that all roads ultimately lead to God by different routes.

The second application is used by skeptics who hold that cultural biases have so seriously blinded us that we can never know the true nature of things. This is Sumner's claim.

Sumner's view, however, is self-refuting. In order for him to conclude that all moral claims are an illusion, he must first escape the illusion himself. He must have a full and accurate view of the entire picture—just as the king could see clearly the blind men and the elephant. The Rajah was in a position of privileged access to the truth, enabling him to correct those who were blind.

Such a privileged view is precisely what Sumner denies. Objective assessments are illusions, he claims, but then he offers his own "objective" assessment. It is as if he is saying, "We're all blind," and then adds, "but I'll tell you what the world really looks like." This is clearly a contradiction.

Society Does Relativism fails on three counts. First, it wrongly assumes that each culture has a unique set of moral values. Second, even if cultures differ radically in their basic moral beliefs, it only shows that there are differing opinions, not that no opinion is correct. It proves nothing about the nature of morality.[10] Third, it denies that objectivity is possible. But the only way to know that our cultural biases blind us to the truth is to have an objective and unbiased point of view.

5

Culture Defining Morality

The second type of relativism we will examine is a bona fide moral thesis because it is prescriptive. While Society Does Relativism merely *describes* the apparent differences in the beliefs of various cultures, Society Says Relativism *prescribes* conduct by telling how one ought to behave. Specifically, people ought to do whatever their "society says" to do.[1]

This view, also known as conventionalism or normative ethical relativism, teaches that each society survives because of consensual moral arrangements that all individuals are obliged to honor. As philosopher Louis Pojman describes it, "There are no objective moral principles, but rather all valid moral principles are justified by virtue of their cultural acceptance."[2] Morality, then, is relative to culture, determined by popular consensus, and expressed through laws, customs, and mores.

Pojman notes that this way of looking at morality has tremendous appeal because of its "live and let live" attitude toward other societies. "[It] seems to be an enlightened response to the sin of ethnocentricity, and it seems to entail or strongly imply an attitude of tolerance toward other cultures."[3]

No Immoral Societies

But Society Says Relativism has serious problems. If culture is both the genesis of and the justification for morality, an odd condition results: If there were no cultures, there would be no morality. Thus if two people live on opposite ends of a desert island with no culture between them, one could kill the other on a whim and never violate any moral rule. This seems counterintuitive, but that is the least of the problems. Others are more substantial.

Conventionalism makes it impossible to criticize another society's practices, no matter how bizarre or morally repugnant they may seem to us. If there is no law above society—no external standard—then that society cannot be judged.

The torture of prisoners by military regimes, the injustice of totalitarian governments, and the apartheid of racist administrations would all be morally benign in this view. One might counter that in many cases these policies are not the will of the people but only of those in power. This rebuttal, though, fails twice.

First, why should one accept that the population at large is the relevant "society" determining morality instead of those who have the power to rule? If one is obligated to obey society, then which society does one obey? This ambiguity is a weakness of conventionalism.

Culture is complex, with many overlapping societies making their claims on us. Behavior acceptable at the gym in the morning is considered gauche at a dinner party later that evening. The moral convictions of one's religious community may be at odds with the demands of the business community. Which group is primary?

Second, the rejoinder also misses the point. Maybe such injustices don't always represent the will of the people, but what if they did? The kangaroo courts of the French Revolution had popular support. And to a great degree, so did the Third Reich. Do we grant French anarchists and German Nazis moral justification on this basis?

Indeed, Society Says Relativism was part of the defense the Nazis presented at Nuremberg. Advancing a notion called legal positivism, the German leadership claimed that the International Military Tribunal had no moral legitimacy to preside over the trials.

In *The Law above the Law,* John Warwick Montgomery describes their argument: "The most telling defense offered by the accused was that they had simply followed orders or made decisions within the framework of their own legal system, in complete consistency with it, and that they therefore ought not rightly be condemned

because they deviated from the *alien value system* of their c
querors" (emphasis added).[4]

But the tribunal did not accept this justification. In the words of Robert H. Jackson, chief counsel for the United States at the trials, the issue was not one of power—the victor judging the vanquished—but one of higher moral law. The tribunal "rises above the provincial and transient," he said, "and seeks guidance not only from International Law, but also from the basic principles of jurisprudence which are assumptions of civilization. . . ."[5]

Society Says Relativism violates our deepest moral intuitions, the foundational "assumptions of civilization." Some things seem wrong regardless of what society dictates, including plundering innocent Jews, pressing them into forced labor, and exterminating them.

If conventionalism is an accurate take on morality, then governmentally sponsored genocide can only be quietly observed, not judged. It cannot even be opposed, because this view requires not only that outsiders remain morally mute in the face of the Holocaust but also that Germans would have been wrong for resisting. Instead they would have had a moral obligation to participate in the murder of innocent people.

Remember, conventionalism teaches that people have an obligation to obey *whatever* their society says to do. All those under the authority of the Third Reich—their ruling society—would have been morally bound to cooperate in genocide.

This leads us to the second problem with Society Says Relativism.

No Immoral Laws

In Society Says Relativism there can be no such thing as an immoral law. Such a concept is an oxymoron—a contradiction in terms. If society is the final measure of morality, then all its judgments are moral by definition.

An attorney once called a radio talk show with a challenge. "When are you going to accept the fact that abortion on demand is the law of the land?" she asked. "You may not like it, but it's the law."

Her point was simple. The Supreme Court has spoken, so there is nothing left to discuss. Since there is no higher law, there are no further grounds for rebuttal. This lawyer's tacit acceptance of conventionalism suffers because it confuses what is right with what is legal.

When reflecting on any law, it seems sensible to ask, It's legal, but is it moral? It's the law, but is the law good; is it just? There appears to be a difference between what a person has the *liberty* to do under the law and what a person *should* do. Conventionalism renders this distinction meaningless. There is no "majority of one" to take the moral high ground. As Pojman puts it, "Truth is with the crowd and error with the individual."[6] This is the tyranny of the majority.

When any human court is the highest authority, then morality is reduced to mere power—either power of the government or power of the majority. If courts and laws define what is moral, then neither laws nor governments can ever be immoral, even in principle.

No Moral Reformation

Another absurd consequence follows from Society Says Relativism. This view makes it impossible to reform the morals of a society. There are actually two problems here; the first is called the reformer's dilemma.

Moral reformers typically judge society from the inside. They challenge their culture's standard of behavior and then campaign for change. But when morality is defined by the present society's standard, then challenging the standard would be an act of immorality. Social reformers would be made moral outcasts precisely because they oppose the status quo.

Corrie ten Boom and other "righteous gentiles" risked their own lives to save Jews during the Holocaust. William Wilberforce sought the abolition of slavery in the late eighteenth century in the United Kingdom. Martin Luther King Jr. fought for civil rights in the United States in the fifties and sixties. In Germany during World War II, Martin Niemöller and Dietrich Bonhoeffer challenged Christians to oppose Hitler.

We count these people as moral heroes precisely because they had the courage to fight for reform. According to Society Says Relativism, however, they are the worst kind of moral criminals because they challenged the moral consensus of their own society.

This view faces another difficulty with the moral improvement of society. Relativism makes the whole concept incoherent. If a society's laws and cultural values are the ultimate standards of behavior, then the notion of moral improvement on a legal or cultural level is nonsense. A social code can never be improved; it can only be changed.

Think of what it means to improve something. Improvement means an increase in excellence by raising to a better quality or condition. How do we know if we have increased the quality of something? Only by noting that some change has brought it closer to an external standard of perfection.

A bowler improves when she raises her average closer to 300, the perfect game. A baseball pitcher increases his skill by decreasing the number of batters he allows on base. If he strikes out every batter, he's attained perfection. In either case, an outside standard is used as the measure of improvement.

To improve a society's moral code means that the society changes its laws and values to more closely approximate an external moral ideal. If no such standard exists, if cultural values are the highest possible law, then there is no way for those standards to be better than what they are at any given moment. They can only be different.

A society can abolish apartheid in favor of equality. It can adopt policies of habeas corpus protecting citizens against unjustified imprisonment; it can guarantee freedom of speech and the press. But according to this view, no one could ever claim that these are moral improvements but only that society changed its tastes.

In Society Says Relativism, the society's standard is the ultimate. There is no objective moral ideal to emulate. Moral *change* is possible, but not moral *improvement.* Improvement means getting better, and there's nothing better—in this view—than any society's current assessment of morality.

No form of culture-based relativism seems defensible. Society Does Relativism is not a true moral thesis, only a flawed observation by anthropologists. Society Says Relativism rules out the possibility of moral critique of any culture, even one's own, because the status quo can never be immoral by definition. Indeed, moral reformers actually turn out to be unethical. This is seriously counterintuitive.

6

Moral Common Sense

Relativism is a bankrupt moral system. There are seven compelling reasons why, which we will explore in the next chapter. Each reason hinges on the validity of a handful of commonsense notions: moral accountability, evil, praise, blame, justice, fairness, moral improvement, moral discourse, and tolerance.

Each concept seems to refer to something real in the world. For example, when a crime is committed, we seek to find the one to blame and praise the prosecutors who put the criminal behind bars. We have debates in the public square on ideals like human rights. We engage in moral discourse to inform and improve our moral conduct. We especially revere the virtue of tolerance.

These notions are so fundamental to our collective human conscience that it seems no sane person would ever reject them. But if this is true, moral relativism has an intractable problem. Indeed, individual ethical or I Say relativism must be false because relativism renders these concepts meaningless and incoherent.

Here's why. Each of these concepts (moral accountability, evil, praise, blame, justice, fairness, moral improvement, moral discourse, and tolerance) depends on some objective, external moral standard for its reality and application. Relativism rejects the premise that such a standard exists. If relativism is true, then we must dismiss these apparently universal moral notions as pointless. But if, in contrast, we have good reason to believe these concepts are true, then some external, objective standard must exist, and relativism must be false.

Everything hinges on the truthfulness of these notions and others like them. But how do we know for certain that these terms refer to true things in the world? We know it by intuition.

A Third Way of Knowing

We know things in a number of different ways. Some things we know through discoveries we make in the physical world when we use our senses to test our environment empirically. After gathering information, we draw conclusions we believe are justified by the evidence. Philosophers sometimes call this *a posteriori knowledge.* Science often employs this empirical method of learning.

Still other things we know through pure reason. We draw inferences based on cause and effect, or we draw conclusions by employing the laws of rationality. If someone offers to show you a square circle for the small charge of two dollars, save your money. Square circles cannot exist because the notion is contradictory. One need not explore the universe to know that such a claim is false. The error is self-evident: contradictory things cannot both be true. There are squares and there are circles, but there are no square circles.

Both of these methods require justification before we can be confident of the results. To demonstrate the truthfulness of a scientific theory, we cite the evidence—the experiments, the observations, the factual data—that leads us to our conclusion. A theory is either good or bad, depending upon how well it is supported by the evidence.

To prove there are no square circles, we appeal to fundamental laws of rationality, like the law of noncontradiction. To test the soundness of an argument, we examine the logical steps that lead us to our conclusion. Are there any fallacies in our line of thinking? If the premises in our argument are accurate and our reasoning is valid, then our conclusion is sound and our results must be true.

There's a third way of knowing, however, that neither needs nor allows any such justification. Intuition is a foundational way of knowing that does not depend on following a series of facts or a line of reasoning to a conclusion. Instead, intuitional truth is simply known by the process of introspection and immediate awareness.

When we use the word "intuition," we mean something specific. We don't mean a policeman's hunch or an experienced stockbroker's sense that the market is headed for a plunge. Those are all specialized insights into circumstances based on prior experience.

The kind of intuition we have in mind is immediate and direct, what the *Encyclopedia of Philosophy* describes as "immediate knowledge of the truth of a proposition, where 'immediate' means 'not preceded by inference.'"[1]

Thomas Aquinas (1225–74) referred to this kind of knowledge when he wrote, "A truth can come into the mind in two ways, namely as known in itself, and as known through another. What is known in itself is like a principle, and is perceived immediately by the mind. . . . It is a firm and easy quality of mind which sees into principles."[2]

Philosophers call this kind of knowing *a priori knowledge* (literally, "from what is prior"), that which one knows prior to sense experience. Ethicist Louis Pojman gives this example to illustrate: If John is taller than Mary and Tom is taller than John, Tom is taller than Mary. He writes: "You do not have to know John, Tom, or Mary. You don't even have to know whether they exist or, if they do, how tall they are in order to know that this proposition is true. You need only whatever experience is necessary to understand the concepts involved, such as 'being taller than.' To believe this proposition a priori, one need only consider it. No particular experience—perceptual, testimonial, memorial, or introspective—is necessary."[3]

Intuitional truth doesn't require a defense—a justification of the steps that brought one to this knowledge—because this kind of truth does not result from reasoning by steps to a conclusion. It's a truth that's obvious upon consideration.

Some people, however, are uncomfortable with this notion, even though there is no other alternative. If you can't know some things without knowing why you know them—if you don't have some things in place to begin with—you can't know anything at all. You can't even begin the task of discovery.

Intuition is the way we start knowing everything. As C. S. Lewis wrote, "If nothing is self-evident, nothing can be proved."[4] We must know certain things immediately—directly—in order to have the tools to learn other things. The mind grasps them instantly, and all inferential knowledge flows from them.

Aristotle put it this way: "Some, indeed, demand to have the law proved, but this is because they lack education; for it shows lack of education not to know of what we should require proof, and of what we should not. For it is quite impossible that everything should have a proof; the process would go on to infinity, so there would be no proof. . . ."[5]

Aristotle argues that certain intuitions must anchor all other knowledge. Say, for example, that I ask you how you know a certain fact. When you offer evidence, I then ask, "How do you know your evidence is reliable?" When you make your defense, I ask, "How do you know *that?*" This same question could be asked again and again, resulting in Aristotle's infinite regress.

If we always have to give a justification for everything we know, knowledge would be impossible because we could never answer an infinite series of questions.[6] It is clear, though, that we do know some things without having to go through the regress. Therefore, not every bit of knowledge requires justification based on prior steps of reasoning. Eventually we are pushed back to something foundational, something we seem to have a direct awareness of and for which we need no further evidence.

Immediate and Obvious

Consider this conversation:

"My hand is injured," I say.

"How do you know it's injured?" you ask.

"Because it hurts."

"How do you know it hurts?"

"Because I feel it."

"But how do you know you feel it?"

Now I'm at an impasse. I don't conclude I feel pain based on other evidence. That knowledge is based on my direct access to my own inner states. Personal sensations are private, immediate, and incorrigible; we cannot be mistaken about them. I may be imagining the injury, but I can't be imagining the imagining; for it isn't possible to think I'm feeling pain and not be feeling it.

We know our own pain—and all of our mental states—through the faculty of immediate awareness or intuition. We simply turn our gaze inward and reflect. This knowledge can't be proved because, on the level of intuition, no further analysis is possible. Analysis makes the complex simple, but if a thing is already simple, it cannot be broken down further.

Basic math is another thing that cannot be proven but is known by intuition. Someone once took us to task on this, suggesting he could scientifically prove two plus two equals four. He took two apples and put them together with two more apples to give a total of four. That was his "scientific" proof.

The math wasn't proven in this case, though; it was simply illustrated with different tokens. A token is some physical representation—a sound, a mark of ink on a piece of paper, an object—that represents the unseen type, which in this case was a number. Consider this illustration.

We could write "two plus two equals four," or "2 + 2 = 4," or substitute apples as our tokens instead of words or numerals. In each case, the math is demonstrated—restated with different tokens—but not actually proven.

We know this to be the case because if this apple demonstration were a true scientific proof, as he attempted, then the experiment would need to be repeated to verify consistent results.

"Repeat the experiment?" one might ask. "That's silly. There's no need to repeat it. The outcome is obvious." That's our point—the answer is obvious to our intuition. No scientific proof is necessary, nor even possible. Indeed, if you disagreed with the answer to the equation, we would be at a complete loss to prove it to you. Either you see it or you don't.

To know something intuitively, incidentally, doesn't always mean we know the facts automatically or inerrantly. Things like apples in groups and a person's height are details of the external world that need to be discovered. Addition and multiplication tables need to be learned. Further, errors in math are common. This, however, is not a mark against intuition but actually evidence for it. If there were no intuition, the errors could never be known, nor could they be rectified.

Thus to know a thing by intuition means that the truth of the proposition is (1) immediately evident, (2) needs no further justification, and (3) is obvious once all the facts are known. Mathematical truth must be learned, but it is justified by an appeal to intuition.

We know many things this way. Intuitional knowledge can be rational, but it can also be moral. There seem to be what philosopher G. J. Warnock called "plain moral facts," or what philosopher Henry Sidgwick termed "moral common sense."

In the Declaration of Independence, our founders referred to certain truths as "self-evident." They needed no defense because they were "self evidenced," so to speak, with their justification coming from within. Upon this foundation these men built their case for the revolution, and we build our case for human rights.

Many of our moral rules are conclusions we arrive at as a result of moral reasoning. Since humans are valuable, for example, we ought not take their lives without proper justification.

Certain moral rules, though, are not conclusions we reach; they are premises we begin with. All moral reasoning must start with foundational concepts that can only be known by intuition, which is why one doesn't carry the burden of proof in clear-case examples of moral truth. People who can't see this, according to philosopher William Lane Craig, are morally handicapped. We shouldn't allow their impaired vision to call into question what is clearly evident.

Those who deny obvious moral rules—who say that murder and rape are morally benign, that cruelty is not a vice, and that cowardice is a virtue—do not merely have a different moral point of view; they have something wrong with them. If somebody says to us, "I think rape is morally acceptable," we're not going to reflect on his alternative morality "tolerantly." Instead, we're going to recommend he get help, fast.

Some will attempt to deny moral intuition by appealing to the inadequate arguments offered for Society Does Relativism discussed earlier. In unguarded moments, though, when an event or situation causes their intuition to rise naturally to the surface, their language gives them away.

When people's "moral common sense" is offended, they are compelled to speak out. They readily pass moral judgment on others, condemning injustice in the courts, or attacking racist governments, for example. This moral intuition provides the foundation for our critique—and later tactical refutation—of I Say Relativism.

7

Relativism's Seven Fatal Flaws

As we have seen, moral accountability, evil, praise, blame, justice, fairness, moral improvement, moral discourse, and tolerance all seem to be concepts that have meaning apparent to our moral common sense. Each is justified by moral intuition, and yet relativism renders them all meaningless. If these moral notions are valid but yet are inconsistent with moral relativism, then relativism must be false.

In this chapter we will explore seven flaws of I Say Relativism that point to its bankruptcy.

Flaw 1

Relativists can't accuse others of wrongdoing. I Say Relativism makes it impossible to criticize the behavior of others, because relativism ultimately denies such a thing as wrongdoing. If you believe morality is a matter of personal definition, then you surrender the possibility of making moral judgments about others' actions, no matter how offensive they are to your intuitive sense of right or wrong. You may express your emotions, tastes, and personal preferences, but you can't say they are wrong.

Nor may you critique, challenge, praise, or fault them. It would be like trying to keep score in a game with no rules or putting a criminal on trial when there are no laws.

To illustrate, relativists cannot object on moral grounds to any form of racism or cultural imperialism if those actions are consistent with the perpetrator's personal moral understanding of what is right and good.

What sense can be made of the judgment "apartheid is wrong" spoken by a relativist? What justification is there to intervene? Certainly not human rights, for there are no objective rights in relativism because there are no rights or wrongs of any kind. As former Attorney General Ramsey Clarke once said, one person's terrorist is another person's freedom fighter.

It would be inconsistent for the same car to sport the bumper stickers "Pro-choice" and "End Apartheid." Relativism is the ultimate pro-choice position, because it legitimizes every personal choice—even the choice to be a racist.

Nor can lying be wrong, even if the lie perverts justice and condemns an innocent person. In fact, there is no real difference between one who is guilty and one who is innocent, because in relativism guilt and innocence are meaningless distinctions.

The notion of a promise is also empty. A promise is not just a statement of intent about the future but also entails the moral obligation to fulfill the intent. That's why changing one's mind is different from breaking a promise, a distinction lost in relativism. No contract could ever have any moral force. Marriage vows would be empty words, providing no comfort or protection for spouses and no stability for families.

There can be no accountability in relativism. Those who answer to themselves ultimately answer to no one of consequence. And this makes it impossible to distinguish relativistic morality from self-interest or ethical egoism.

Further, if morality is an individual call, and if moral wrong is the kind of error for which punishment seems to be justified, then all punishment would have to be approved by the individual responsible for the "immoral" conduct.

This is the first law of relativism: When right or wrong are a matter of personal choice, we surrender the privilege of making moral judgments on others' actions. But if our moral intuition rebels against these consequences of relativism—if we're sure that some things must be wrong and that some judgments against another's conduct are justified—then relativism is false.

Flaw 2

Relativists can't complain about the problem of evil. The reality of evil in the world is one of the first objections raised against the existence of God. The common argument says that if God is absolutely powerful and ultimately good, he would deal with evil. But since evil exists, God appears too frail to oppose it or too sinister to care.

The entire objection hinges on the observation that true evil exists. The only way one can have this complaint about God is if evil is "out there" as an objective feature of the world. Evil can't be real if morals are relative to the subject.

Relativism is inconsistent with the concept that true moral evil exists because it denies that some things are objectively wrong. Evil as a value judgment marks a departure from some standard of moral perfection. But if there is no standard, there is no departure. As C. S. Lewis notes, a portrait is a good or bad likeness depending on how it compares with the "perfect" original.

Relativism denies such a standard. This was a serious problem for Lewis: "My argument against God was that the universe seemed so cruel and unjust. But how had I got this idea of *just* and *unjust?* A man does not call a line crooked unless he has some idea of a straight line. What was I comparing this universe with when I called it unjust? . . . Of course, I could have given up my idea of justice by saying it was nothing but a private idea of my own. But if I did that, then my argument against God collapsed, too—for the argument depended on saying that the world was really unjust, not simply that it did not happen to please my private fancies" (emphasis in the original).[1]

If relativism is true, the objection against God based on evil vanishes.[2] There is no true evil to discuss, only differing opinions about what is pleasant or unpleasant, desired or not desired.

This point was made clear in the movie *The Quarrel.* The main characters, Hersh and Chiam, grew up together but separated because of a dispute about God and evil. Then came the Holocaust, and each thought the other had perished. Reunited by chance after the war, they become embroiled once again in their boyhood quarrel. Hersh, now a rabbi, offers this challenge to the secularist Chiam: "If there's nothing in the universe that's higher than human beings, then what's morality? Well, it's a matter of opinion. I like milk; you like meat. Hitler likes to kill people; I like to save them. Who's to say which is better?

"Do you begin to see the horror of this? If there is no Master of the universe, then who's to say that Hitler did anything wrong? If there is no God, then the people that murdered your wife and kids did nothing wrong."

The approach many relativists take at this point is confused. First, they say that the Holocaust was evil and ask why God would allow such depravity. Later, when the tables turn and their own behavior is in question, they argue that morality is merely a matter of opinion. This reduces their earlier objection to, How could a good God allow things that are contrary to my opinion?

We mentioned earlier that people belie their denial of moral intuitions when they are betrayed by their own language. Sociologist Os Guinness explains: "Have you ever heard someone say, 'God damn it,' and really mean it? Most people use that phrase only casually as trivial blasphemy, but some people don't. Why? They face evil which is so evil that, however they've been trained, they've got to say '*God* damn it' even if they are atheists. . . . Doesn't everything in our studies tell us that nothing is absolute, all is relative? Play those ideas out to the end of the line, if you like. There are still experiences so evil in life that people say, 'God damn it.' They know intuitively that here is something so wrong it needs an absolute judgment, whether or not they have a philosophical basis."[3]

Moral relativism and objective evil are strange bedfellows. They couldn't possibly both be true at the same time. If morality is ultimately a matter of personal tastes, like preferring steak over broccoli or brussels sprouts, the argument against God's existence based on the problem of evil vanishes. Relativists must surrender this objection.

If, however, it seems legitimate to raise the issue of evil in the world, then relativism can't be true.

Flaw 3

Relativists can't place blame or accept praise. Relativism renders the concepts of praise and blame meaningless, because no external standard of measurement defines what should be applauded or condemned.

Without absolutes, nothing is ultimately bad, deplorable, tragic, or worthy of blame. Neither is anything ultimately good, honorable, noble, or worthy of praise. It's all lost in a twilight zone of moral nothingness.

Relativists are almost always inconsistent here. They seek to avoid blame but readily accept praise. C. S. Lewis notes that our habits of welcoming praise and of making excuses to avoid blame evidence our deep commitment to objective morality: "The truth is, we believe in decency so much—we feel the Rule or Law pressing on us so—that we cannot bear to face the fact that we are breaking it, and consequently we try to shift the responsibility. For you notice that it is only for our bad behavior that we find all these explanations. It is only our bad temper that we put down to being tired or worried or hungry; we put our good temper down to ourselves."[4]

Psychologist B. F. Skinner argues in *Beyond Freedom and Dignity* that humans are simply biological machines whose conduct is determined by a mixture of biology and environment. In *Walden II,* his description of the brave new world founded on principles of behavior modification, the concepts of praise and blame are portrayed as completely meaningless. Morality is a fiction.

In like fashion, relativists must remove the words *praise* and *blame* from their vocabularies. But if the notions of praise and blame are valid, then relativism must be false.

Flaw 4

Relativists can't make charges of unfairness or injustice. Justice and fairness are two more concepts that don't make sense in a world devoid of moral absolutes. Under relativism, these notions are incoherent for two reasons.

First, the words themselves have no meaning. Both concepts dictate that people receive equal treatment based on an external standard of what is right. This outside standard, though, is the very thing repudiated by relativists. After all, how can there be justice or fairness if there are no moral requirements to be just or fair? It's not wrong to punish an innocent person, nor is it immoral to release the guilty.

Second, there is no possibility of true moral guilt. Justice entails, among other things, punishing those who are guilty. Guilt, however, depends on blame, which we have seen cannot exist. If nothing is ultimately immoral, there is no blame and subsequently no guilt worthy of punishment.

People give away their true intuitions about justice and fairness by their language. "A nation may say treaties do not matter," says Lewis, "but then, next minute, they spoil their case by saying that the particular treaty they want to break was an unfair one. But if treaties do not matter, and if there is no such thing as Right and Wrong . . . what is the difference between a fair treaty and an unfair one?"[5]

If relativism is true, then there is no such thing as justice or fairness. Both concepts depend on an objective standard of what is right. If the notions of justice and fairness make sense, however, then relativism is defeated.

Flaw 5

Relativists can't improve their morality. With moral relativism, moral improvement or reform is impossible. Relativists can change their personal ethics, but they can never become better people.

How can one get "better"? Moral reform implies an objective rule of conduct as the standard to which we ought to aspire. But this rule is exactly what relativists deny. If there is no better way, there can be no improvement.

Further, there is no motive to improve. Relativism destroys the moral impulse that compels people to rise above themselves, because there is no "above" to rise to, ethically speaking. Why change our moral point of view if it serves our self-interest and feels good for the time being?

In relativism, by definition one's ethics can never be more "moral" at one time than another. Morals can change, but they can never improve. If, however, moral improvement seems to be a concept that makes sense, then relativism can't be true.

Flaw 6

Relativists can't hold meaningful moral discussions. Relativism makes it impossible to discuss morality. What's there to talk about? A meaningful ethical dialogue can be held only when moral principles are seen as universal action guides.

Ethical discourse involves comparing the merits of one view with another to find which is best. But if morals are entirely relative and all views are equal, then no way of thinking is better than another. No moral position can be judged adequate or deficient, unreasonable, unacceptable, or even barbaric.

Twentieth-century English philosopher A. J. Ayer agrees, arguing that ethical statements are meaningless because they are not empirically verifiable: "We find that argument is possible on moral questions only if some system of values is presupposed."[6]

Ayer's own view, called emotivism, denies that ethical statements are anything more than raw expressions of emotion. As such, they have no more content than words like "Wow!" or "Yuck!" "If a sentence makes no statement at all, there is obviously no sense in asking whether what it says is true or false. And we have seen that sentences which simply express moral judgments do not say anything. They are pure expressions of feeling and as such do not come under the category of truth and falsehood."[7]

If Ayer is right, then moral education is impossible, because the words themselves are meaningless. One can't even have a moral dispute. Yet quarrels seem to entail meaningful moral discussions, as Lewis points out: "Quarreling means trying to show that the other man is in the wrong. And there would be no sense in trying to do that unless you and he had some sort of agreement as to what Right and Wrong are; just as there would be no sense in saying that a footballer had committed a foul unless there was some agreement about the rules of football."[8]

If ethical disputes make sense only when morals are objective, then relativism can only be consistently lived out in silence. For this reason, it's rare to meet a thorough-going relativist. Most are quick to impose moral rules like, It's wrong to push your morality on others.

The best example of consistency I've encountered came from a caller on my radio show.[9] I'd talked to Jim, a relativist, many times before. I was hoping a fair question would show the foolishness of his view. Jim surprised me with his honesty.

"Jim," I said, "are you saying there's no moral difference between feeding a starving child and murdering him?"

"I'm saying the question doesn't even make any sense," he responded. "It's as meaningless as talking about a snake with legs. It's nonsense, so you can't even get started."

Jim understood that if relativism is true, all moral categories are meaningless. He knew that any attempt at moral discourse would be silly, like talking about a snake with legs.

The only course of action truly consistent with moral relativism is complete silence. If you view all morality as relative and you're consistent, you can't ever make a moral recommendation.

This puts relativists in an untenable position, caught coming and going. If they speak, they surrender their relativism. If they do not speak, they surrender their humanity. It's inhuman to be mute in the face of egregious evil, to be silent in the presence of flagrant injustice.[10]

Those who believe that ethical truth is relative cannot say anything further that is morally meaningful. But if the notion of moral discourse makes sense intuitively, then moral relativism is false.

Flaw 7

Relativists can't promote the obligation of tolerance. Finally, there is no tolerance in relativism, because the relativists' moral obligation to be tolerant is self-refuting.

The principle of tolerance is considered one of the key virtues of relativism. Morals are individual, relativists argue, and therefore we ought to tolerate the viewpoints of others and not pass judgment on their behavior and attitudes.

It should be obvious that this attempt fails through contradiction.[11] To relativists, tolerance means, "I (morally) ought to tolerate the moral opinions and behavior of others who disagree with me. I (morally) should not try to interfere with their opinions or behavior."[12]

If there are no objective moral rules, however, there can be no rule that requires tolerance as a moral principle that applies equally to all. In fact, if there are no moral absolutes, why be tolerant at all? Why not force my morality on others if it's in my self-interest and my personal ethics allow it?

Relativists violate their own principle of tolerance when they do not tolerate the views of those whose morality is nonrelativistic. They only tolerate those who hold their ethical viewpoint. They are, therefore, just as intolerant as any objectivist appears to be.

The principle of tolerance is foreign to relativism. If, however, tolerance seems to be a virtue and we owe a measure of respect to those who differ with us, then relativism can't be true.

The Sum of All Flaws

What kind of world would it be if relativism were true? It would be a world in which nothing is wrong—nothing is considered evil or good, nothing worthy of praise or blame. It would be a world in which justice and fairness are meaningless concepts, in which there would be no accountability, no possibility of moral improvement, no moral discourse. And it would be a world in which there is no tolerance.

Moral relativism produces this kind of world. The late Dr. Francis Schaeffer's remark could well apply to relativists, who ". . . have both feet firmly planted in mid-air."

Part 3

Relativism and Education

8

Values Clarification

Public debate on moral issues is not exempt from the influence of moral relativism, which seems to be lurking behind most rhetoric in America. People seem to assume that no objective moral values apply to all people in all times and in all places. Thus they begin and end their public moral judgments with such qualifying phrases as "It's only my personal opinion," "Of course I am not judging anyone's behavior," or "If you think it's all right, that's okay, but I'm personally against it."

Having defined and critiqued moral relativism in parts 1 and 2, we move in parts 3 and 4 to exploring its role and effect in society in the areas of education, law, and public policy.

What's Dogmatic?

In his best-selling book *The Closing of the American Mind,* Allan Bloom writes: "The relativity of truth [for college students in American culture] is not a theoretical insight but a moral postulate, the condition of a free society, or so they see it. . . . The point is not to correct the mistakes and really be right; rather it is not to think you are right at all. The students, of course, cannot defend their opinion. It is something with which they have been indoctrinated. . . ."[1]

According to Bloom, people who dogmatically maintain that there is no truth are relativists who have become close-minded to the possibility of knowing the truth, if in fact it exists. To understand what Bloom means, consider this dialogue (based loosely on a real-life exchange) between a high-school teacher and her student Elizabeth:

Teacher: Welcome, students. This is the first day of class, and so I want to lay down some ground rules. First, since no one has the truth, you should be open-minded to the opinions of your fellow students. Second . . . Elizabeth, do you have a question?

Elizabeth: Yes, I do. If nobody has the truth, isn't that a good reason for me *not* to listen to my fellow students? After all, if nobody has the truth, why should I waste my time listening to other people and their opinions? What's the point? Only if somebody has the truth does it make sense to be open-minded. Don't you agree?

Teacher: No, I don't. Are you claiming to know the truth? Isn't that a bit arrogant and dogmatic?

Elizabeth: Not at all. Rather I think it's dogmatic, as well as arrogant, to assert that no single person on earth knows the truth. After all, have you met every person in the world and quizzed them exhaustively? If not, how can you make such a claim? Also, I believe it is actually the opposite of arrogance to say that I will alter my opinions to fit the truth whenever and wherever I find it. And if I happen to think that I have good reason to believe I do know the truth and would like to share it with you, why wouldn't you listen to me? Why would you automatically discredit my opinion before it is even uttered? I thought we were supposed to listen to everyone's opinion.

Teacher: This should prove to be an interesting semester.

Another Student: (blurts out) Ain't that the truth. (the students laugh)

As this exchange shows, moral relativism has had a pervasive influence in our culture, especially on the American education system.

Moral Mayhem

Focusing on the public-school system, former Secretary of Education William Bennett explains the moral crisis in that institution by contrasting the concerns of teachers in two different eras: "Over the years teachers have been asked to identify the top problems in America's schools. In 1940 teachers identified them as talking out of turn; chewing gum; making noise; running in the hall; cutting in line; dress code infractions; and littering. When asked the same question in 1990, teachers identified drug abuse; alcohol abuse; pregnancy; suicide; rape; robbery; and assault."[2]

During the thirty-year period of 1960 to 1990, "there has been a 560 percent increase in violent crime; more than a 400 percent increase in illegitimate births; a quadrupling in divorces; a tripling of the percentage of children living in single-parent homes; more than a 200 percent increase in the teenage suicide rate; and a drop of 75 points in the average SAT scores of high-school students."[3]

We do not believe it is a coincidence that the increase of moral mayhem described by Bennett corresponds with an increased acceptance of moral relativism. In fact, relativism has been officially incorporated in the educational curriculum, known as values clarification.

Clarifying Their Values

From the mid-sixties to the early seventies, the values-clarification curriculum was introduced into the public-school system (though many private schools used it as well). It is one of the most famous and influential programs of moral education found in elementary and secondary schools.

Developed in the sixties by Louis Raths, Sidney Simon, and other educators, values clarification "is not concerned with the *content* of people's values, but the *process of valuing.*" According to Simon, this approach "does not teach a particular set of values. There is no sermonizing or moralizing. The goal is to involve the students in practical experiences, making them aware of *their own* feelings, *their own* ideas, *their own* beliefs, so that the choices and decisions they make are conscious and deliberate, based on *their own* value systems [emphasis in the original]."[4]

The foundational assumption of values clarification, however, is not the student's own. Instead, the notion that morality is exhaustively described by one's own personal feelings, ideas, beliefs, and values comes from Simon and Raths. Theirs is not a neutral point of view but rather the view of morality known as relativism.

This leads values-clarification advocates into contradiction, as Paul Vitz, professor of psychology at New York University, points out: "The theorists clearly believe that values clarification is good. . . . They criticize traditional teaching of values as 'selling,' 'pushing,' and 'forcing one's own pet values.' But when it comes to the value of their own position, relativism has conveniently disappeared, and they push their moral position with their own sermons."[5]

This lack of neutrality can be seen in two examples that follow.

"Neutral" Values in Hawaii

My youngest brother raised his children in Hawaii.[6] At the time, the public-school system there conducted exercises in values clarification in which the students were encouraged to develop their own beliefs about morality. The teacher was "neutral," explaining to the students that it was up to them to formulate their own moral conclusions to ethical dilemmas.

The children were asked to solve a problem. An aged man had taken the life of his seriously ailing wife to put her out of her misery and was therefore being tried for murder. Should he be punished for his "mercy killing," or should he go free?

My brother made a visit to the school to register his concern, but the teacher defended the practice. "We're not pushing our views or imposing our values," he said. "We're careful to let the students know that it's up to them to decide what to do. This is 'value-free' instruction. We're neutral."

My brother pointed out that the teacher's approach was anything but neutral. "You're telling my children that when they face the hard questions of right or wrong, when they're confronted with the most difficult problems of morality, there are no guidelines. There are no absolutes. There are no rules. You're teaching my kids that when they must decide critical issues of right and wrong, it's simply up to them."

How "value-free" is this instruction? Take another example, which follows.

The Value of Cheating

Philosopher Christina Hoff Sommers exposes the moral confusion of values clarification in a true story she relates: "One of my favorite anecdotes concerns a teacher in Newton, Massachusetts, who had attended numerous values clarification workshops and was assiduously applying its techniques in her class. The day came when her class of sixth graders announced that they valued cheating and wanted to be free to do it on their tests. The teacher was very uncomfortable. Her solution? She told the children that since it was her class and since she was opposed to cheating, they were not free to cheat. 'In my class you must be honest, for I value honesty. In other areas of your life you may be free to cheat.'"[7]

Think about this response for a moment. Does the teacher's solution follow from the instruction on values clarification she has just given to her students? Of course not. If the teacher values honesty, then *she* should be honest without imposing her values on her students. They should still decide for themselves, which they had.

At best, the instructor is stuck in a contradiction. When faced with the destructive consequences of relativism, she falls back into imposing her morality on her students—the very thing she's been teaching against.

At worst, the teacher instructs that power is the ultimate element in morality, that might makes right: "I give the grades. If you cheat, I'll flunk you." Technically, this is called the fallacy of *argumentum ad baculum,* or to paraphrase Mao Tse-tung, "persuasion from the barrel of a gun."[8]

The Myth of Neutrality

Values clarification is not neutral. Vitz points out five areas of bias. First, its exercises embody the moral ideology of a small, liberal segment of America. Second, its values are relative to individual tastes. Third, possible solutions to the moral dilemmas posed to students are limited to the most liberal options. Fourth, the exercises focus on the individual in isolation from family and society. And fifth, morality is construed simply as self-gratification. "It is a simple-minded, intellectually incompetent system."[9]

What are values clarification exercises meant to teach? That there are difficult ethical circumstances in which the lines are not clear and the solutions are ambiguous? We already know that. No, these exercises go further. They imply that because some circumstances are ethically ambiguous, there are no ethical certainties at all.

Values clarification aggressively promotes a particular ethical view—moral relativism. It uses ethical ambiguities to encourage agnosticism about universal moral rules. By posing extremely difficult problems to children untutored in ethical decision-making, values clarification destroys their confidence in moral absolutes.

9

no morals

Relativism's Offspring: Political Correctness and Multiculturalism

Moral relativism has made a tremendous impact on some recent movements in higher education that come under the general heading of *political correctness* (PC).

PC assumes moral relativism in most of its manifestations.[1] Indeed, much of PC thinking has been influenced by another form of relativism, *epistemological relativism.* The word *epistemology* refers to one's view or theory of knowledge—one's explanation of how human beings come to know things. Before looking at the PC issue, we first need to understand this other type of relativism.

Objective or Relative

Epistemological relativism sees knowledge as relative, and objective truth as nonexistent. To believe in objective truth, in contrast, is to affirm that some claims about the world are true or false regardless of what others perceive to be true. In chapter 2 we defined *objec-*

tive and *subjective* as they relate to morality; below, philosophers Peter Kreeft and Ron Tacelli clarify what these terms mean when applied to knowledge:

> 1. The word *objective* in the phrase "objective truth" does not refer to an unemotional, detached, or impersonal attitude. Truth is not an attitude. Truth is not *how* we know, truth is *what* we know.
>
> 2. *Objective* does not mean "known by all" or "believed by all." Even if everyone believes a lie, a lie is still a lie. "You don't find truth by counting noses."
>
> 3. *Objective* does not mean "publicly proved." An objective truth could be privately known—for example, the location of a hidden treasure. It could also be *known* without being *proved*; to know is one thing, to give good proofs or reasons for our knowledge is another.
>
> What *objective* means in "objective truth" is "independent of the knower and his consciousness." "I itch" is a subjective truth; "Plato wrote the *Republic*" is an objective truth. "I don't want to be unselfish" is a subjective truth; "I ought to be unselfish whether I want to or not" is an objective truth.[2]

The fact that objective truth exists does not mean that people's subjective perceptions, prejudices, biases, or faulty theories do not get in the way of it. Neither does it mean that anyone who claims to have objective truth really has it. In fact, to affirm that some perceptions and claims are flawed and that we can progress in our knowledge of the world after detecting these flaws *assumes* the reality of objective truth. We cannot say that someone is wrong unless we have some notion as to what is right—what is objective truth.

PC—Political, but Correct?

Utter the words "political correctness" or "politically correct" today and you will undoubtedly provoke vitriolic denunciations, accusations of brutal caricature or false hysteria, or perhaps even congratulations. What is this movement that prompts such an emotional response?

PC can be loosely defined as a web of interconnected, though not mutually dependent, ideological beliefs that have intensified our cultural, gender, class, and racial differences in the name of diversity. Challenging the traditional nature of the university and its curriculum, PC has evolved in some circles into an unchallenged orthodoxy that calls into question our standards of excellence and views about justice, truth, and the objectivity of knowledge, including moral knowledge. Typically it falls to the left of the political spectrum, although some of its harshest critics are on the political left,[3] just as many critics of McCarthyism were on the political right.

PC is often linked with *multiculturalism,* a philosophy of education that may be more difficult to define precisely than the concept of political correctness. Philosopher Steven Yates argues that multiculturalism primarily takes two forms, one that he calls *weak multiculturalism* and the other *strong multiculturalism.*

Weak multiculturalism holds certain values to be grounded in our common humanity: the understanding, appreciation, and recognition of those who have been ignored or oppressed. It sees objective moral goods—such as justice and liberty—for which we should strive and uphold. And whenever an injustice has occurred, we should do our best to rectify it.[4] So, for example, if particular writers, scholars, scientists, or historical figures have been ignored because of their race, ethnicity, or gender—and not because of a lack of quality—the academic community should recognize them by incorporating their work in the curriculum.

Weak multiculturalism also believes that we should study and understand the diverse cultures and subcultures of our country and the world. We should search out and discover knowledge and truth wherever it may be found.

Weak multiculturalism, however, is not cultural egalitarianism—the belief that all cultures are equal. It understands that some cultures, like some individuals, have discovered more knowledge and truth than others. Each culture need not be "represented" in the curriculum, but rather truth and knowledge must be taught, wherever they have originated.

Strong multiculturalism, in contrast, is much more closely aligned with PC. It makes at least two philosophically suspect assumptions. First, that no single culture, thinker, or group has discovered the objective "truth" about anything, because no universal truth exists. Take, for example, the comments by a task force on multicultural education and diversity commissioned for the president of California State University at Long Beach: "The problem with 'exclusive' curricula is that they equate the values of a dominant group with 'universality,' and falsely present the experience of a dominant group as a formula for all other groups."[5]

The second assumption of strong multiculturalism is that every judgment can be reduced to a "cultural perspective." Barbara Herrnstein-Smith, English professor at Duke University and former president of the Modern Language Association, seems to support this claim: "There is no knowledge, no standard, no choice that is objective. . . . Even Homer is a product of a specific culture, and it is possible to imagine cultures in which Homer would not be very interesting."[6] Consequently, if no standard, knowledge, or choice is objective, then moral claims are relative as well.

These assumptions presuppose the two philosophical perspectives mentioned at the beginning of this chapter: epistemological relativism and moral relativism. These views also form the philosophical basis for an intellectual movement known as *postmodernism,*[7] whose assumptions have been applied to questions of truth, culture, religion, and politics.

Although the purpose of this book is not to analyze this recent movement, our critique, if successful, undermines the intellectual basis for it. If the assumptions of postmodernism fail to withstand philosophical scrutiny, then the basis of strong multiculturalism collapses. Weak multiculturalism, however, remains unaffected.

Self-Refuting Claims

Epistemological relativism—the view that knowledge is relative—can be seen in multiculturalists' assumption that "every judgment can be reduced to a 'cultural perspective.'" But this assumption, like the assumptions of moral relativists we explored earlier, is self-refuting. Philosopher J. P. Moreland defines self-refutation: "When a statement fails to satisfy itself (i.e., to conform to its own criteria of validity or acceptability), it is self-refuting. . . . Consider some examples. 'I cannot say word in English' is self-refuting when uttered in English. 'I do not exist' is self-refuting, for one must exist to utter it. The claim 'there are no truths' is self-refuting. If it is false, then it is false. But if it is true, then it is false as well, for in that case there would be no truths, including the statement itself."[8]

Other examples of self-refuting claims include "Language cannot convey meaning," "It is true that it is impossible to make objective claims about the world," "Every statement I make is a falsehood," and "All truth is relative."

How then is the assumption that "every judgment can be reduced to a 'cultural perspective'" self-refuting? Because it itself is a judgment. Using their own terms, the judgment is merely a cultural perspective, something that cannot be objectively and universally true.

Multiculturalists, however, put forth this assumption as universally true because they claim it about *every* judgment. Hence if it is objectively and universally true that "every judgment can be reduced to a 'cultural perspective,'" then this statement is false because it asserts that "every judgment can be reduced to a 'cultural perspective.'"

More sophisticated defenders of the PC position claim that their view is not self-refuting because they deny that they espouse epistemological relativism. They argue that although no objective universal norms of knowledge and morality exist, objective norms are valid within such interpretive communities as cultures, civilizations, nations, and ethnic heritages.

Defenders of the PC mindset Jung Min Choi and John W. Murphy explain: "Each community, accordingly, values certain norms. Therefore, some norms may be irrelevant in a specific community, because behavior is not random but is guided by expectations that are known by every competent member of a region. Exhibiting just any behavior would certainly result in a negative sanction. Within an interpretive community the idea that anything goes [i.e., relativism] is simply ridiculous, for all norms do not have equal validity."[9]

Another supporter of PC, Betty Jean Craige, says that since "there is no external reality subject to partition and definition, then different viewpoints generate different understandings of events."[10]

According to these advocates of PC, their view is not relativistic because it affirms that each community has its own absolute norms of knowledge and morality. These norms, however, do not apply to other communities. Several examples will illustrate.

Take communities X and Y. Community X believes it is morally permissible to torture babies for fun but community Y maintains that this practice is morally wrong. According to Craige, Choi, and Murphy, no moral norms transcend communities X and Y by which we can say that Y's view of torturing babies is better than X's view.

Or consider this. Suppose that the people in community X believe that the best method of making major medical decisions is to consult a Ouija board and the zodiac. So if Dr. Jones recommends an appendectomy for Mr. Smith but the Ouija board says no, it is best for Mr. Smith not to undergo the procedure.

Members of community Y used to believe the same thing as the people in X, but they have discovered through numerous experiments that consulting the zodiac or a Ouija board is no better than guessing, flipping a coin, or just plain luck. The people in Y now rely on the science behind their medicine. For that reason they have far fewer dead patients than community X.

If Craige, Choi, and Murphy are correct that norms of knowledge are community-relative, then we have no basis to assert that community Y's decision-making process is better than community X's view. It is clear, however, that Y's perspective is truer than X's perspective and thus results in a larger body of knowledge.

Even though they may claim otherwise, the position defended by Craige, Choi, and Murphy *is* relativism, because it denies that universal norms of knowledge and morality transcend diverse cultures.

Failure on Three Counts

True or Not True

This more sophisticated defense of epistemological relativism fails for other reasons as well. First, it is similar to its simpler cousin in that it is self-refuting. Craige's claim that since "there is no external reality subject to partition and definition, then different viewpoints generate different understandings of events" is either true or not true.

If her statement is true, then it is a claim about reality, and this means that an external reality *is* subject to partition and definition. If her statement is not true, then it is merely one of many "different viewpoints [which] generate different understandings of events." And this means that an external reality *may be* subject to partition and definition. Once again we have a self-refuting statement.

Crossing Boundaries

Second, the defenders of the PC position seem to *presuppose* the very positions they denounce. For example, Choi and Murphy argue for the concept of interpretive communities but then defend the work of Duke University professor Stanley Fish:

> Sociologists of various hues have *verified a long time ago* what Fish is saying. Symbolic interactionists, for example, have illustrated that *persons* evaluate their actions with regard to their respective "reference groups." Therefore, in terms of a single city, very different pockets of norms may be operative. To understand what deviance means in each circumstance, *a priori definitions of normativeness must be set aside.* For *norms are embedded in symbols, signs, and gestures that may be very unique and restricted to a specific locale.*
>
> Upon crossing one of these relatively invisible boundaries, an individual quickly learns which behaviors are acceptable. This diversity, moreover, has not resulted in the disaster that conservatives predict. Yet navigating through this montage of norms *requires interpretive skill, tolerance, and an appreciation for pluralism* [emphasis ours].[11]

According to Choi and Murphy, *sociologists verify* the PC perspective that knowledge and morality are relative. Apparently sociologists, or at least the sociologists who verify PC, are not restricted by their interpretive communities. And their claim that sociologists verify the PC perspective as true means that one *has knowledge* about reality. But as we have seen, PC advocates deny this.

If these sociologists are restricted by their interpretive communities, they lack an objective knowledge of reality. How then can Choi and Murphy claim that the PC perspective has been "verified"? Choi and Murphy must presuppose that one can have knowledge of the real world in order to verify the PC perspective.

If the PC perspective is correct, the observations put forth by these sociologists cannot be true claims about the world. Thus the statements of Choi and Murphy that "a priori definitions of normativeness must be set aside," that "norms are embedded in symbols, signs, and gestures that may be very unique and restricted to a specific locale," and that "navigating through this montage of norms requires interpretive skill, tolerance, and an appreciation for pluralism" are not true.

If, however, these are indeed true claims about the world, then the PC perspective is false, since we can have objective knowledge of the world.

As we have seen, the appeal to sociologists who "verify" the PC view presupposes that the PC view is false. And this is another way of showing that their view is self-refuting.

In addition, defenders of PC assume certain objective moral norms. For instance, Choi and Murphy maintain that interpretive skill, tolerance, and appreciation for pluralism are virtues by which one navigates "through this montage of norms." But by this claim they are offering objective moral guidelines that apparently transcend any particular interpretive community. Everyone, they say, should have these virtues while navigating through *all* of the interpretive communities.

In other words, Choi and Murphy are requiring that all people, regardless of their interpretive community, abide by certain universal objective moral norms. If not, then members of those interpretive communities that don't accept these norms need not abide by them. These could be Nazi Germany, a skin-head commune, or a group of sociopaths.

Obviously this is absurd, for any moral theory that cannot account for the objective wrongness of Nazism, neo-Nazism, or callous disregard for others cannot be taken seriously.

Indoctrinated Dogmatism

Third, PC is unjustifiably dogmatic and thus close-minded to the possibility that truth exists. In his influential work on the crisis in our universities, *The Closing of the American Mind,* Allan Bloom writes about the widespread belief among students that truth is relative. "The students, of course, cannot defend their opinion. It is something with which they have been indoctrinated."[12] By dogmatically asserting that there is no truth, the naive student and the PC advocate become close-minded to the possibility of even knowing the truth if it does exist.

This closed attitude explains why the view of epistemological relativism by PC supporters differs significantly from traditional philosophical skepticism. PC advocates are actually much closer to solipsists, those who hold that reality is only what individuals perceive in their minds.

The skeptics for the most part do not deny that truth exists. Rather they claim that we cannot be sure when and if we have the truth, or at least that we are incapable of providing a rational justification for truth. PC advocates, however, are *not* skeptics. They are dogmatists who simply assert that objective truth cannot be known. Unlike skeptics, they are emboldened, not humbled, by their ignorance.

As we have shown, the view of epistemological relativism put forth by PC advocates fails because it is self-refuting, presupposes what the view denies, and is unjustifiably dogmatic.

Binding Moral Principles—or Not

Moral or value relativism logically follows from epistemological relativism: If knowledge is relative to interpretive communities and moral claims are knowledge claims,[13] then moral claims are relative to interpretive communities. According to this view, no single particular moral perspective is universally binding. Since the majority of our book responds to this viewpoint, we will only briefly in this chapter raise a few problems with moral relativism as it relates to the question of political correctness.

Stanley Fish exemplifies this relativism in his claim that freedom of speech, as found in the First Amendment of the U.S. Constitution, has no inherent value: "I think . . . that people cling to First Amendment pieties because they do not wish to face what they correctly take to be the alternative. That alternative is *politics*, the realization . . . that decisions about what is and is not protected in the realm of expression will rest not on principle or firm doctrine, but on the ability of some persons, to interpret—recharacterize or rewrite—principle and doctrine in ways that lead to the protection of speech they want heard and the regulation of speech they want silenced. . . . In short, the name of the game has always been politics, even when (indeed, especially when) it is played by stigmatizing politics as the area to be avoided."[14]

According to Fish, no moral principles are binding on all persons everywhere and in every place. There is simply *politics*, the cultural perspective of the elite who control the interpretive community. In other words, like the teacher in chapter 8 who forbade cheating, *might makes right.* Outside of one's own political institutions, no objective right or wrong transcends all the interpretative communities by which to judge others or their behavior.

But this position fares no better than epistemological relativism. The value relativist, like the epistemological relativist (of course, they could be the same person, such as in the case of Fish), believes that value judgments, like knowledge claims, can be reduced to the perspective of a culture or an interpretive community. This view has many problems. Consider just the following.

Insufficient Moral Work

First, value relativism undermines the moral strength of PC advocates' entire enterprise. That is to say, if value judgments are *merely* cultural, then the value of PC is *merely* cultural. But then why do PC proponents judge as morally wrong such institutions as slavery and apartheid? Couldn't someone respond to this judgment as being "ethnocentric"? After all, people in cultures that practice slavery and apartheid believe these practices to be correct. Who are the PC followers that they have the right to judge?

Now, of course we believe that apartheid and slavery are morally wrong. But we don't think that the PC perspective (and its view of multiculturalism, as currently defined) does the moral work sufficient to make such a judgment.

Although space does not permit us to present an alternative moral perspective for grounding multiculturalism,[15] several exist. For example, a robust view of natural law (such as the view defended by Martin Luther King Jr. in his "Letter from the Birmingham Jail"[16]) can rescue PC and multiculturalism from the philosophical problems inherent in value relativism.

Transcending Views

Second, some defenders of PC celebrate the normative value of tolerance as an integral part of the PC enterprise. According to Choi and Murphy, the purpose of tolerance is to help us navigate "through this montage of norms."[17]

But this view has several problems. For example, the call to tolerance by most defenders of PC presupposes the existence of at least one nonrelative, objective value that transcends the "montage of norms": tolerance. Tom Beauchamp observes:

> If we interpret normative relativism as *requiring* tolerance of other views, the whole theory is imperiled by inconsistency. The proposition that we ought to tolerate the views of others, or that it is right not to interfere with others, is precluded by the very strictures of the theory. Such a proposition bears all the marks of a *non-relative* account of moral rightness, one based on, but not reducible to, the cross-cultural findings of anthropologists. . . . But if this moral principle [of tolerance] is recognized as valid, it can of course be employed as an instrument for criticizing such cultural practices as the denial of human rights to minorities and such beliefs as that of racial superiority. A moral commitment to tolerance of other practices and beliefs thus leads inexorably to the abandonment of normative relativism.[18]

Choi and Murphy seem to affirm other objective moral norms that apparently transcend interpretative communities, since these norms are employed to justify the entire PC enterprise:

> . . . this is the moral imperative of PC: Foster and protect the integrity of difference.[19]

> The interpretative schemes that constitute persons' identities, experiences, cultures, and relationships, for example, should be allowed to flourish.[20]

> No norm, belief, or viewpoint should be allowed to upset the balance between narratives.[21]

> In short, PC consists of theories and practices that are designed to end injustices based on sex, race, class, and other social variables.[22]

An Invalid Argument

Third, Fish, like so many in the political-correctness movement, confuses disagreement between political interests with a proof-of-value relativism. Fish accurately points out that people will defend, employ, and interpret certain principles when those principles serve their interest. Put differently, many of what seem to be moral disputes are actually merely political disputes.

Fish has a point here. For example, when some people do not get what they want, whether an extra piece of pie, a love interest, or a government entitlement, they may claim that the situation is "unfair." They may or may not have been treated unfairly in reality, but that they didn't get what they want does not in itself entail unfair treatment. After all, a burglar who is apprehended is not getting what he wants.

Fish may have a point, but his argument does not prove value relativism. His observation that political interests are really political disputes does not lead logically to the statement that no objective moral principles exist. Fish's argument can be put this way:

1. Some moral disputes are really political disputes.

Therefore,

2. There are no objective moral principles.

Since the conclusion can be false *and* the premise true, the conclusion does not follow from the premise. Hence, Fish's case for value relativism is based on an invalid argument.

To understand better why Fish's argument fails, consider the following example:

1. Mr. Jones and two hundred other people were at the scene of the crime.

Therefore,

2. Mr. Jones is guilty of the crime.

Since the premise can be true, that Mr. Jones as well as two hundred other people were at the scene of the crime, while the conclusion is simultaneously false, that Mr. Jones is *not* guilty of the crime, this argument is invalid. Fish's argument shares the same flaw. Although his premise is certainly true, it is not enough to prove his conclusion.

Suppose, however, that Fish changed his premise to the stronger claim that "*all* moral disputes are really political disputes." Even so, it still would not follow that no objective moral principles exist, since Fish's revised premise would describe how human beings behave; it would not give evidence that moral principles do not actually exist. For it is possible that human beings are fundamentally selfish creatures who, though intuitively aware of objective moral principles, most often or always choose what is expedient to keep themselves in political power. After all, if every nation were ruled by a tyrant, it would not follow that tyranny is morally justified. Fish commits the fallacy of confusing what *is* with what *ought* to be.

It seems incredible and implausible that *all* moral disputes are really political disputes. Fish isn't omniscient, so how can he possibly know and evaluate *all* moral disputes?

10

On the Road to Barbarism

As one might guess, the institutionalizing of epistemological and moral relativism has produced some practical consequences, mostly negative. In this chapter we will examine the impact of political correctness on our culture as it replaces traditional notions of excellence with an ethic of power.

The Consequences of a Flimsy Dogma

According to some who adhere to strong multiculturalism and political correctness, to emphasize the classics of Western civilization in a college curriculum while not giving equal time to other traditions is "Eurocentric." That is, it is wrong to treat the great works of Western culture as more important than the works of other cultures.

This perspective assumes that the values of greatness and excellence are wholly relative to one's culture or even one's ethnicity. According to this view, it is racist (or "ethnocentric") to believe that one culture or civilization has realized more truth about the universe than other cultures or civilizations.

For example, some multiculturalists argue that an African-American student who studies only Dead White European Males (DWEMS), such as Plato, Aristotle, and Galileo, will not do as well as if she studied the greats of African culture. This is why Afrocentric scholar Molefi Kete Asante claims that wherever people of African descent may live, "we respond to the same rhythms of the universe, the same cosmological sensibilities. . . . Our Africanity is our ultimate reality. . . . There exists an emotional, cultural, psychological connection . . . that spans the ocean."[1]

More Self-Refuting Ideas

This view is seriously flawed. First, it is self-refuting. Its proponents say that cross-cultural judgments are wrong because such notions as "greatness" and "excellence" are culturally relative. On the one hand, if this statement is true, then the PC proponents' judgment about the wrongness of making cross-cultural judgment is itself culturally relative. We can therefore reject it as being inconsistent with *our* cultural practice of judging other cultures.

On the other hand, if the PC proponents' judgment is legitimate, then not all assessments of greatness and excellence are culturally relative, since they are arguing that theirs is *better* than a Western one. In any event, the PC advocates' position is self-refuting.

Promoting Racism

Second, the view that one can understand the ideas of one's own ethnic or racial group more easily than those of another culture may serve to excuse and reinforce racist behavior and attitudes. For example, how would a black person be able to present this view to a white audience, since the white audience would, according to this outlook, have difficulty comprehending the speaker? But then the white audience, if racist, could excuse its racism on the basis that it only understands the ideas of those in its own racial group. Put another way, if all values are culturally and ethnically relative, then racism cannot be morally judged as objectively and universally evil. This is absurd.

Truth Is Free

Third, when PC advocates argue that you are racist if you believe that some cultures have contributed more to human progress than others, aren't they actually the ones putting forward racism? After all, they seem to assume that racial superiority can be inferred from superior accomplishment.

This is obviously flawed. $E=mc^2$ is not Jewish simply because it was discovered by Albert Einstein, a Jew. Some cultures have simply done better than others because they stumbled upon ideas that facilitate progress. Other insights result from philosophical views about the universe, humanity, and knowledge; others are rooted in a society's geographical location, economic needs, or religious perspective.

Once the ideas and insights of an individual or group are disseminated, anyone can employ them. No one culture owns its accomplishments; they belong to everyone. When the knowledge is out there, we can all access it. There is no inexorable link to race or ethnic origin.

For example, even though primarily Western scholars have developed modern physics, it is not inherently Western. If a primitive thinks he can jump off a thousand-foot precipice and fly because the totem told him he can, he will die. His death is not caused by Eurocentric science but by his ignorance of the nature of reality Western scientists articulate.

Having said all of this, we must emphasize that if significant accomplishments have been ignored, we should redress that injustice—not because of the race or ethnicity of the thinker but because of the importance of the ideas.

George Reisman, an economist at Pepperdine University, has made similar observations. He argues that the trends toward "multicultural education" and "diversity" as well as critiques of "Eurocentric" or "Western" values are misguided and ill-informed.

For one thing, these trends imply that all cultures have contributed to human progress and knowledge equally. Reisman argues that this is false, since Western values—whether scientific, philosophical, economic, or moral—have proved to be vastly superior. Those societies that have embraced Western values, whether geographically in the Far East or in the West, reveal this.

In addition, Western civilization is open to everyone, since it constitutes a body of knowledge and values that is not linked inexorably to any race, nationality, or region of the globe. For these reasons,

Reisman contends that multiculturalism is a new form of racism because it reduces a matter of the intellect to a matter of racial or ethnic membership.[2] Reisman explains how this dangerous doctrine results from cultural relativism:

> The equivalence of all cultures, the equivalence of civilization and savagery, is the avowed claim of the doctrine of cultural relativism, which has long been accepted by practically the whole of the educational establishment. It in turn is a consequence of the still older, more fundamental doctrine that there is no objective foundation for values—that all value-judgments are arbitrary and subjective. The new racists are now merely cashing in on this view and attempting to apply it on the largest possible scale, in the process substantially altering the manner in which subjects are taught. Today's educational establishment has fewer compunctions about putting absurd ideas into practice probably because of the deteriorated state of its own education. [3]

As we have argued earlier, objective moral truth is not contingent on race, culture, or ethnicity. Thus we can condemn *both* Western imperialism and headhunting in Africa. And objective truth, whether moral or epistemological, also permits us to break free from our cultural prejudices. We can therefore embrace truth and excellence wherever we find it, even if Athens and Jerusalem have more of it than West Hollywood or Greenwich Village.

Strong multiculturalism denies us the ability to make these cross-cultural judgments. It also forces us to tolerate barbarism in order to avoid being accused of ethnocentrism. On the authority of flimsy dogma, it requires that we become close-minded to the possibility of objective truth, all in the name of inclusiveness, tolerance, and sensitivity.

Without Truth, There Is Power

PC advocates deny the existence of objective knowledge and morality, and thus see no point in employing moral suasion and logical argument to convince their fellow citizens that their viewpoint is correct. Their only means available is therefore using the instruments of political power, such as coercion, intimidation, marginalization, and name-calling. To put it philosophically: Ideas are not the power by which to change the world, but rather, the world's ideas are changed by power.

Consider the following real-life examples.

University of Pennsylvania—Nobody in Professor Dolfman's class in legal studies at the University of Pennsylvania could identify where the term "servitude" could be found in the American Constitution, so Dolfman commented that there were "ex-slaves" in the class who should have an idea. "I don't know if I should have used the term," Dolfman recalled, "but it got students to think of the Thirteenth Amendment right away."

Shortly afterwards, a few minority students came up to Dolfman and accused him of racial insensitivity. A second charge against Dolfman was that he had once told a black student to change his pronunciation from "de" to "the." Dolfman said that he met with the students, and apologized if they had taken offense. "I told them that I understood and shared their concerns, that I am Jewish and during *seder* we pray: When we were slaves unto Pharaoh." Dolfman also pointed out that it would be important for students, in courtroom argument in later years, to speak in a clear and comprehensible manner.

"They seemed to understand," Dolfman recalled, and the matter was dropped for a few months. But after that, during Black History Month, it was brought up again and again, Dolfman said, "to illustrate just how bad things are at Penn."

The adrenaline generated by the Black History Month rhetoric brought about a demonstration by minority students, several dozen of whom occupied Dolfman's class and prevented him from teaching. "They read a document of indictment to my students," Dolfman said. President Sheldon Hackney met with Dolfman and asked him to refrain from public comment, even to abstain from defending himself against accusations. Then Hackney joined the ranks of the accusers, telling the campus newspaper that conduct such as Dolfman's was "absolutely intolerable." Dolfman was pressured to issue what he termed a "forced apology," and to attend "racial awareness" sessions on campus. The university subsequently decided not to renew Dolfman's teaching contract for a year. Dolfman is now back at Penn, a chastened man. "The message has been driven home very clearly," Dolfman said. "You can't open your mouth on these issues now without fear of being humiliated."[4]

Marrietta College—A student wrote an article in the student newspaper in which he referred to lesbianism as "deviant." He was charged with "sexual harassment" by a campus lesbian. The administration intended to expel him from the private Ohio college. [The Individual Rights Foundation] interceded with a threat of litigation based upon his contractual rights under the student code as well as the First Amendment principles based on the college's acceptance of government funding. The Board of Trustees reconsidered the administration's action, and the student was allowed to remain without disciplinary action.[5]

Cohen v. San Bernardino Valley College—A professor of creative writing was accused of "sexual harassment" as a result of assigning his class to write on the subject of pornography and discussing Jonathan Swift's "A Modest Proposal." He has been threatened with loss of tenure and direct firing.[6]

A number of similar cases have been documented in which students and faculty have been charged because of their words.[7]

The Harassment of Speech Codes

These incidences occurred because many colleges and universities have instituted rules forbidding "racist," "sexist," or "homophobic" speech—another manifestation of the PC philosophy of power. Conservative religious believers are especially concerned about these codes because some rule out a respectful and academically serious presentation of religious views.

At the law school of the State University of New York at Buffalo, the faculty adopted a resolution that cautioned students not to make "remarks directed at another's race, sex, religion, national origin, age, or sexual preference," including "ethnically derogatory statements, as well as other remarks based on prejudice or group stereotype."[8]

A policy at the University of Connecticut is typical of many throughout the United States. It "interprets as 'harassment' all remarks that offend or stigmatize women or minorities. Examples of violations of the University President's Policy on Harassment, for which the penalty ranges from a reprimand to expulsion, include 'the use of derogatory names,' 'inconsiderate jokes,' and even 'misdirected laughter' and 'conspicuous exclusion from conversation.'"[9]

These college speech codes have numerous problems, three of which follow.

Inconsistency in Instruction

First, institutions that look the other way in virtually every other area of personal student conduct, such as eating habits, exercise, driving safety, consensual sex, and the use of alcohol and drugs, now issue speech codes. They are telling students not to speak in a way that may be perceived as disparaging about another's appearance, sexual practices, or cultural background. Evidently, on some college campuses it is permissible to behave like a tramp but impermissible to be called one.

Limiting Speech of All Kinds

Second, and most importantly, although most of the codes forbid speech that is racist, sexist, homophobic, or creates a hostile work environment, little is done to define and keep free speech that is intellectually engaging but sometimes controversial. This especially affects Christian students and faculty. Their views, such as on the exclusivity of the Christian faith and the immorality of homosexual conduct, may subject them to institutional punishment and public ridicule.

The question about these codes is not whether academic institutions should forbid verbal harassment and other types of behavior. They should. Rather the concern is that the intellectual liberty of those who have views that are not politically correct will be limited. Thus civil libertarians view speech codes as an attempt to silence unpopular ideas in the name of limiting "harassment."

Consider the following examples, which would seem to violate almost all of the speech codes we perused but are nevertheless intellectually controversial topics:

"Western civilization has contributed more to human progress than all the indigenous peoples of North America combined."

"Male homosexual intercourse (anal sex) is inherently unhealthy."

"Women tend to be more emotional than men."

"Dedicated Christians tend to be morally better people than followers of Ayn Rand."

"Homosexuality violates natural moral law."

"The metaphysical worldview of certain branches of Hinduism is irrational."

"Homosexuality is psychologically dysfunctional."

This limitation on freedom of expression violates the longstanding Western tradition of the university as the locus of free expression. As we have seen, this results in a chilling effect on the free expression of controversial or unpopular ideas on college campuses.

A Climate of Incivility

Third, the groups these speech codes are supposed to protect tend to have a heightened sensitivity. A climate of incivility results, because those whose views are dissimilar to those who are protected are accused of being insensitive and mean-spirited. And thus campus speakers, professors, and students who hold such views are treated with disrespect and, in some cases, are verbally harassed or even physically threatened.

Unfortunately, such reactionary behavior is not reprimanded by college administrators nor is it prosecuted under existing speech codes. We believe this lack of action results because the codes were written to protect only certain groups with left-wing political leanings. So, for example, a white male or a white woman (such as Jeanne Kirkpatrick, Christina Hoff Sommers, or Elizabeth Fox-Genovese) or a member of a minority group (such as Thomas Sowell or Clarence Thomas) who dares to challenge the PC orthodoxy is not protected.

Presumed Guilty

Take the following example. Late one evening in 1993 a student at the University of Pennsylvania was studying in his dorm room. A small group of women was making noise outside his window, evidently disturbing his ability to study. After a few minutes, the student shouted out his window to the women, "Shut up, you water buffaloes!"

At the time, the student did not realize that the women were African-Americans. Because of their race, however, his comment was interpreted as a racial epithet. The student was soon charged with violating the University of Pennsylvania's speech code, although these charges were subsequently dropped.

Of course, no moral person would countenance the use of racial epithets. We find them disgusting and in violation of our Christian ethics. But the point here is that instead of giving the student the benefit of the doubt, as well as due process, his guilt was presumed. The young women belonged to a protected class and the young man did not; he was a white male.

Objective knowledge and objective morality were dispensed with in academic discourse, and so it did not matter whether the women had a racial slur intentionally and maliciously hurled at them, *they perceived such a slur.* Their perception, not what really happened, is what mattered.

Also, because it is power and not objective morality that dictates how wrongs should be righted, the young women could have hurled a racial slur at the young man, since only the "oppressor" can be racist or sexist (heterosexual white males) and not the "oppressed" (women, people of color, homosexuals).

If you find this difficult to believe, consider the following statements:

- Former *New York Times* columnist Anna Quindlen writes: "Hatred by the powerful, the majority, has a different weight and often very different effects than hatred by the powerless, the minority. . . . Being called a honky is not in the same league as being called a nigger."[10]
- Filmmaker Spike Lee states: "Black people can't be racist. Black people don't have the power to keep whites from getting jobs or the vote. To me, racism is the institution. You got to have power to do that."[11]
- Rap singer Sister Souljah asserts: "You can't call me or any black person anywhere in the world a racist. We don't have the power

to do to white people what white people have done to us. And if we did, we don't have that low-down dirty nature."[12]

- "Racism connotes power," explains Coramae Richey Mann, a black scholar, "and in only a few instances can a minority person have a quantum of power; since they lack institutional power, it is definitely impossible for American minorities to be identified as racist."[13]
- In her textbook *Racism and Sexism,* academic and activist Paula Rothenberg writes that "while an individual person of color may discriminate against white people or even hate them, his or her behavior cannot be called racist. Racism requires prejudice plus power."[14]

The young man at the University of Pennsylvania was wrong in what he said, but not because one of "the powerful" (a white male) was denigrating the "powerless" (black women). Rather, the reason is based on commonsense morality: It is morally wrong for a young man to speak that way in public to other people, especially young women. And it would have been equally wrong if the young women had yelled nasty sentiments at the young man.

We have *moral* responsibilities to other people in our community because they are people, regardless of their race, ethnicity, gender, or lot in life. According to the Christian and Jewish view of humanity, all people have inherent dignity because they are made in the image of God. And thus we should show respect to and concern for those of both genders and all races and nationalities.

PC advocates appear to defend the absurd because they see history as a series of unprosecuted crimes that can only be redeemed if we are appropriately sensitive to the legacy of the victims. But history is much more complex. It is a dynamic process of conflicting ideas shaped by philosophy, geography, religion, and politics. This process results in everything from the grandeur of human genius, compassion, and love to the dehumanization of persons by means of the gulag, gas chamber, crusade, and chains. If there is such a thing as original sin (and we believe there is), it has been equitably distributed. But we must not forget, "Where sin increased, grace abounded all the more."[15]

When Might Makes Right

To show the state of things on some college campuses, consider what happened to me (Frank) on October 22, 1996. Earlier that fall I had been invited by the Associated Students of California State University, Los Angeles, to participate in a debate on the California Civil Rights Initiative (CCRI), an initiative to ban both preferential treatment and discrimination based on race or gender in state government hiring. I supported the initiative, which passed on November 5, 1996. It has been implemented only after its opponents lost a challenge in federal court and the U.S. Supreme Court refused to hear the case.

Having participated in a number of panel discussions and debates on assorted topics, I accepted the invitation. I understood the volatile nature of the issue but assumed that since the debate was going to be conducted at a university, it would be held in a civil and respectful manner. Nothing could have been further from the truth.

My opponent for the debate, Rudy Acuna, directs the Chicano Studies program at Cal State, Northridge. A long-time political activist, Acuna on October 22 had no interest in civil discourse. During my opening comments, Acuna walked off the podium and left the room for a period of time. Evidently he was not interested in a serious discussion on a serious issue.

Rather it seemed he was more concerned with entertaining his followers, mostly students who didn't seem to understand what is involved in intellectual disputation. They were rude, mean-spirited, hateful, and unthinking.

Prior to the debate, my wife, Frankie, who was there with her friend Gretchen Passantino, went to the back of the room to get some coffee. She overheard one man, who looked like he was dressed in gang regalia, say to a couple of his friends, "We came here looking for a fight and we're going to get one." This made Frankie a little nervous. She told me later that she was glad that I didn't point her out to the audience during the debate.

Gretchen heard Mr. Acuna tell a group of students before the debate, "Who is this Beckwith guy anyway? He's just some white philosopher. What does that tell you about what he has to say?" This is not the way a professor should speak publicly to students about a fellow academic. He was not telling these students to listen and reflect but rather to be unthinking bigots. He was undermining the possibility for civil discourse.

In my opening comments I explained the meaning of CCRI and how it would force the California government to espouse the nobility of the civil-rights vision that has been buried for years. Nearly three decades of policies, however well intended, have wrongly equated achieving certain unjustified numerical ends (such as having 50 percent of all civil engineers be women because women make up half the population) as sufficient justification for treating individuals unjustly on the basis of their race or gender. For example, Ms. A gets job X over a more-qualified Mr. B since women are "underrepresented" in this profession.

In addition, I made the point that CCRI would not affect affirmative action policies that do not rely on gender or racial preferences. Thus opponents of CCRI who claim that its passing would eliminate all affirmative action are mistaken. Although all preferential-treatment policies are cases of affirmative action, not all cases of affirmative action are cases of preferential treatment, just as all New York Yankees are baseball players but not all baseball players are New York Yankees.

I also presented an argument for why preferential policies harm those they are intended to help. During segments of my talk Acuna's groupies hissed. When I stepped down from the podium I received light applause.[16]

Mr. Acuna then took the podium. He started out by saying that he was not there to debate. He stated that anyone, including me, who is against affirmative action of any kind is a racist and no different than David Duke.

He then spoke about an evil conspiracy involving major conservative think-tanks and corporate interests that is intended to destroy opportunities for minorities, especially Hispanics. Although he provided no evidence for such a conspiracy, he had his groupies in a lather. In fact, the lone security guard provided by the university was cheering him on. I did not feel very safe.

Acuna did everything *except* deal with CCRI and the arguments for it. He did not put forth a moral, legal, or social case for affirmative action or preferential treatment. During the question-and-answer period, he continued to engage in guilt by association and name calling, at one point calling me "young" and "naive" and at another engaging his constituency in the "farmer's clap." He was clearly there to engage in demagoguery, pure and simple.

After the debate, Frankie, Gretchen, and I were escorted out the back by a group of College Republicans, who thought that there may be trouble if we walked out through the center of the crowd. Prior to leaving the room, however, an Acuna partisan approached me and asked, "Are you a Native American?" Because of my facial features and dark complexion (which I get from my mother who is Italian-American), I am sometimes asked if I am a member of a minority group. When I said, "No," the man said, "I figured that. 'Beckwith' is a dirty, filthy, English name."

He went on to badger and insult me, in front of what appeared to be the man's daughter and wife. The students surrounding them seemed enthused by his ridicule.

He then told me, "You're going to give us our land back, you filthy English."

I replied, "I don't want to disappoint you, but since I can't even get a traffic ticket fixed in L.A., I don't think I'll be able to get you your land back."

I was then whisked away by the College Republicans.

The disrespect and anti-intellectualism I encountered at Cal State L.A. is typical of the climate that has been created on college campuses by those, such as Professor Acuna, who have abandoned academic discourse for political posturing. This is what happens when the search for truth is abandoned for politics and replaced by an ethic of might makes right. The barbarians are inside the gates.[17]

Part 4

Relativism and Public Policy

11

Relativism and the Law

Education is not the only sphere of public life that has been affected by moral relativism. In this chapter we turn to the sphere of law and especially to how relativism has allowed our public culture and the courts to dismiss cavalierly those views that do not assume it.

Those who employ relativistic premises when arguing about these issues do so by appealing to personal subjective relativism (or I Say Relativism). As we have seen, this view holds that because there is no objective good, the state or community should allow all people to decide for themselves what is good; goodness, like beauty, is in the eye of the beholder. Proponents of this form of relativism appeal to fairness and personal autonomy to justify their position.

These people claim that it would not be fair for the state or community to judge one person's lifestyle choice as good and another's as bad. They see any such judgment as a violation of the individual's personal autonomy to choose whatever he or she believes is "the good."

One could say that fairness and personal autonomy are "objective moral norms" and that people who appeal to these concepts are therefore not moral relativists. But this would be missing the point. Relativists are *not* supporting fairness and autonomy as universally true prescriptions; rather they are putting them forth as *instrumental* goods that the state must practice so that individuals can pursue their own personal desires—that is, to choose what they feel is good. John

Rawls, the most influential contemporary philosopher of liberal political thought, has presented a sophisticated defense of such a view.[1]

Rawlsian Principles of Justice

According to Rawls, a just state (or government) results from those principles people would choose if they knew nothing about who they are or what they will become—that is, whether rich or poor, black or white, homosexual or heterosexual, short or tall, male or female, and so on.[2]

To employ Rawls's terminology, the principles of justice are those agreed to by parties in "the original position" behind "a veil of ignorance." His original position refers to an imaginary place and time where there is no government; his veil of ignorance is an imaginary situation in which no one has any knowledge of themselves or their futures.

In other words, the principles of justice are arrived at by means of a social contract agreed upon by all the "unbiased" parties. These princples would ensure full political and social freedom and a minimum standard of financial entitlement just in case, for example, one is not well-off, not naturally gifted, or holds unpopular opinions.

Rawls's principles of justice therefore have little or nothing to do with the good, the true, or the beautiful. Instead they are principles for ensuring economic entitlement and for preventing conflict between individuals choosing their subjective preference.[3]

Rawls does claim that his view of state neutrality does not prevent certain conceptions of the good, such as religious or philosophical views, from influencing public policy. Such conceptions, however, must not conflict with the principles of justice.[4] Also, the principles of justice would exclude conceptions of the good that violate personal autonomy, meaning that traditional positions on such issues as same-sex marriage, physician-assisted suicide, or abortion would not get a hearing in such a state.

We are not saying that the state should never be neutral on anything. For example, the state should not take a position on infant baptism or prefer one race over another or one religion over another. Rather it should discourage prejudice and encourage free expression of one's religious tradition.

The state is justified, however, in prohibiting practices of certain religious traditions or philosophical viewpoints that violate those institutions and principles deemed essential to the nurturing of public virtue. Polygamy, same-sex marriage, incestuous marriage, and child sacrifice are examples of practices that can be prohibited according to this view.

What we are concerned about here is the appeal to state neutrality being accepted at face value without critical reflection. For this appeal is really not neutral at all but presupposes a particular view of personal morality and social philosophy that is relativistic and anticommunitarian. It also encourages views of the human person that are philosophically naturalistic—the outlook that human nature has no nonphysical aspect such as a soul and that human beings have no transcendent purpose.

We will take a sobering look at some recent court decisions that seem to reinforce personal relativism and philosophical naturalism as the official creed of American legal and popular culture.

Matters of Life and Death

Contemporary jurisprudence is headed in a troubling direction. It seems that absolute personal autonomy and personal subjective relativism are becoming the primary dogmas by which courts, especially the U.S. Supreme Court, decide issues of great moral and social importance. Let's look at how they have approached issues of life and death.

In 1992 the Supreme Court upheld *Roe v. Wade* (1973) as a precedent in considering the case *Planned Parenthood v. Casey.* In its decision the Court departed from its 1973 appeal to the right to privacy and instead grounded abortion rights in an appeal to near absolute autonomy. This autonomy it sought to ground in the Fourteenth Amendment of the U.S. Constitution. "Our law affords constitutional protection to personal decisions relating to marriage, procreation, family relationships, child rearing, and education. . . . These matters, involving the most intimate and personal choices a person may make in a lifetime, choices central to personal dignity and autonomy, are central to the liberty protected by the Fourteenth Amendment. At the heart of liberty is the right to define one's own concept of existence, of meaning, of the universe, and of the mystery of human life. Beliefs about these matters could not define the attributes of personhood were they formed under compulsion by the State."[5]

Although political philosopher Hadley Arkes says that "this is the kind of sentiment that would ordinarily find its place within the better class of fortune cookies,"[6] this passage from *Casey* was taken to heart by Judge Stephen Reinhardt of the Ninth Circuit Court of Appeals. In the March 6, 1996, ruling of *Compassion in Dying v. Washington,* he affirmed not only a constitutional "right to die" but also called the state's motivation for banning physician-assisted suicide "cruel": "Not only is the state's interest in preventing such individuals from hastening their deaths of comparatively little weight, but its insistence on frustrating their wishes seems cruel indeed."[7]

Two years prior to this ruling, Judge Barbara Rothstein of the U.S. District Court in Seattle struck down the state's ban on physician-assisted suicide, employing the logic of *Casey:* "Like the abortion decision, the decision of a terminally ill person to end his or her life 'involves the most intimate and personal choices a person can make in a lifetime,' and constitutes a 'choice central to personal dignity and autonomy.'"[8]

In supporting this decision, philosopher Ronald Dworkin makes a similar appeal, emphasizing the state neutrality articulated in *Casey:* "Our Constitution takes no sides in these ancient disputes about life's meaning. But it does protect people's right to die as well as live, so far as possible, in the light of their own intensely personal convictions about 'the mystery of human life.' It insists that these values are too central to personality, too much at the core of liberty, to allow a majority to decide what everyone must believe."[9]

These decisions are particularly troubling because they concern a case in which the citizens of Washington reaffirmed their state's long-time prohibition of assisted suicide. In 1991 the people of Washington reasserted through a statewide referendum their community's dedication to the sanctity of human life and a commitment to maintaining the moral integrity of the medical profession. But the pro-euthanasia organization Compassion in Dying sued the state of Washington and won in two courts, with both courts saying that the law violated the Fourteenth Amendment of the Constitution.

Consider also a New York case, *Quill v. Vacco,* decided in the Second Circuit Court of Appeals. In that case the court ruled that "the state of New York violates the equal protection clause of the Fourteenth Amendment with its prohibition of assisting suicide. By permitting patients to refuse treatment at the end of life, but not allowing physician-assisted suicide, the state unfairly treats similarly situated persons."[10]

The court in this case did not take seriously the traditional distinction between passive (letting die) and active (killing) euthanasia. It concluded that no moral distinction divides the two, and thus for the state to permit one (passive euthanasia) but not the other (active euthanasia)[11] violates the Equal Protection Clause of the Fourteenth Amendment.

Like the Ninth Circuit and the District Court in Seattle, the Second Circuit appealed to *Casey.* Writing for the majority, Judge Miner asked, "What concern prompts the state to interfere with a mentally competent patient's 'right to define [his] own concept of existence, of meaning, of the universe, and of the mystery of human life,' when the patient seeks to have drugs to end life during the final stages of a terminal illness?" The answer, according to Judge Miner, is "None."[12]

Philosopher Russell Hittinger, a critic of the case, explains the judge's reasoning: "[G]iven two patients, each of whom can define the meaning of the universe, the state of New York violates equal protection when it allows one to 'define' himself by having treatment withdrawn [passive euthanasia] while it forbids the other to 'define' himself by requesting that a physician assist his suicide [active euthanasia]."[13]

These cases were decided in federal appeals courts on matters of constitutional law and are therefore legally significant. In the words of Hittinger, they are "authoritative renderings of the fundamental law."[14]

The U.S. Supreme Court seems for the time being to have rejected this interpretation of *Casey,* for on June 26, 1997, it overturned federal appeals court rulings in both *Compassion* and *Quill.* Nevertheless, this interpretation finds acceptance among some of the more influential social and legal philosophers, such as John Rawls and Ronald Dworkin.

Sexual Politics

In May 1996 the U.S. Supreme Court in *Romer v. Evans* ruled that the state of Colorado could not prohibit the state or any of its jurisdictions from granting protected status to homosexuals. Groups that have protected status are those such as African-Americans and women. Society has tried to remedy the discrimination they have suffered by the use of such public policies as antidiscrimination laws, affirmative-action policies, and special scholarships to government schools.

The Court in its decision overturned Colorado's Amendment 2, which had been passed by referendum in 1992 with 54 percent of the popular vote. The Colorado ballot contained the following question: "Shall there be an amendment to Article II of the Colorado Constitution to prohibit the state of Colorado and any of its political subdivisions from adopting or enforcing any law or policy that provides that homosexual, lesbian, or bisexual orientation or conduct, or relationships, constitutes or entitles a person to claim any minority or protected status, quota preference or discrimination?"

The Court's majority decision, written by Justice Anthony Kennedy, maintains that Amendment 2 is unconstitutional because it violates the Equal Protection Clause of the Fourteenth Amendment. Kennedy draws this conclusion on the basis that the Colorado amendment singled out homosexuals as an identifiable group and withheld from them the opportunity to receive special protections. Thus homosexuals were denied equal protection under the law since other groups, such as minorities, women, and the handicapped, were still permitted to enact statutes to receive special protections. And because the amendment, according to Kennedy, had no rational basis, it raises "the inevitable inference that the disadvantage is born of animosity toward the class of persons affected."[15]

In this decision the Court redefined the principle of "treating people equally" to include "treating people's behavior equally." Justice Kennedy illustrated this clearly when he cited Justice John Marshall Harlan's famous dissent from the separate-but-equal case *Plessy v. Ferguson* (1896): The Constitution "neither knows nor tolerates classes among citizens."

Kennedy comments: "Unheeded then, those words now are understood to state a commitment to the law's neutrality where the rights of persons are at stake."[16] It is one thing to embrace "equality of all people"; it is quite another to translate that into "equality of all lifestyles." Given Justice Kennedy's definition of "equality," it is wrong for the law both to permit one to marry one's neighbor's sister and at the same time to forbid one to marry one's own sister.

The philosophical ground for this reasoning, and for the reasoning in all the cases mentioned in this chapter, is that personal subjective relativism and absolute autonomy are the primary basis for deciding moral issues that touch on public policy. Therefore any legislation that presupposes a notion of what is morally good cannot be rational. The reasoning behind this belief is that the state ought not to concern itself with "the good" ("a commitment to the law's neutrality") and that such legislation would violate each person's right to pursue what each believes and chooses to be good for oneself (absolute autonomy).

Thus any moral opposition to homosexuality reflected in public policy is *by definition* irrational and must be "born of animosity," as Justice Kennedy puts it. Consequently, the legal and philosophical principles set forth by the Court imply a new constitutionally sanctioned view about the nature of human sexuality and its place in community—sexual egalitarianism. This is the belief that no sexual practice is more or less good than any other as long as all the participants exercise their personal autonomy.

Couple this conclusion with Justice Kennedy's recent claim that it is a religious belief to hold that "there is an ethic and morality which transcend human invention,"[17] and the Court now has another "constitutional" basis for affirming sexual egalitarianism—and forbidding the prohibition of same-sex marriage.

Thus the Court may now appeal both to the Fourteenth Amendment and to the Establishment Clause of the First Amendment. To assert that the state ought to prefer a certain lifestyle, such as heterosexual marriage and the raising of children, because it is inherently good and part of the natural order of things would be, according to Justice Kennedy, "transcendent" and therefore "religious."

Given the Court's espousal of sexual egalitarianism, it would not be surprising to see the debate over polygamy being reopened or debates arising over the constitutionality of incest laws and the age of sexual consent.

Problems with the Law

No Form of Redress

The courts today seem to be saying that moral considerations, the community, and certain views of what it means to be human are to be discarded and replaced with "absolute autonomy." They also seem to be limiting the people's legal tools of the legislature and the referendum. People have traditionally fashioned the moral and social parameters of their communities through such means. They have also used these tools to redress what is perceived as harmful to the public good or to the character-shaping institutions, such as the family, medicine, school curricula, the arts, and higher education.

Because of this reasoning, the courts will continue to misunderstand or ignore the intentions and purposes of legislation passed to sustain institutions of great civic, community, and social value, such as traditional marriage and family life. Political philosopher Hadley Arkes's comments on the *Romer* case are instructive in this regard:

> The Amendment [in Colorado] merely sought to preserve for people, in their private settings, the freedom to honor their own understandings on the matter of homosexuality. The Amendment licensed no criminal prosecutions directed at gays and lesbians, and it withdrew from homosexuals no protections of the law. Still, the Court overturned this move by the people of Colorado, acting in their sovereign capacity, to shape their fundamental law. . . . With Amendment 2, the people of Colorado had decided simply to withhold endorsement or favoritism: The coercions of law would not be used to punish those people who bore moral objections to homosexuality. And yet, this perspective, reflected in the law, was characterized by the Court now

> as an "animus," a form of blind prejudice that could not justify itself in the name of rational purpose. . . . In a stroke then—and without the need to marshal reasons—the Court could pronounce the traditional moral teachings of Judaism and Christianity as empty, irrational, unjustified.[18]

According to Arkes, the amendment passed overwhelmingly in order to prevent future and current government bodies from passing ordinances that provide "a club for the law in meting out public humiliations for people who hold moral and religious objections to homosexuality." Arkes tells of the case of "the wife of a shopowner in Boulder, Colorado, [who] had given a pamphlet on homosexuality to a gay employee. For that offense, she was charged under the local ordinance on gay rights, and compelled to enter a program of compulsory counseling."[19]

A Lack of Neutrality

Contrary to their intent, when courts appeal to absolute autonomy as a "neutral position," they violate their primary reason for this appeal. Recall the Supreme Court's assertion from *Casey:* "At the heart of liberty is the right to define one's own concept of existence, of meaning, of the universe, and of the mystery of human life. Beliefs about these matters could not define the attributes of personhood were they formed under compulsion by the State."

Here the Court is asserting that since personal autonomy is more important than the metaphysical question of who and what is a person, the state should remain neutral on such ultimate philosophical questions. The problem, of course, is that this appeal to autonomy is far from neutral. Rather it assumes a view of reality, and of the person in particular, that is secular, anticommunitarian,[20] and metaphysically libertarian.

That is to say, the Court answers an ultimate philosophical question consistently with the Court's own philosophical predilections. And these are far from neutral.

For when the Court affirms "personal autonomy," it apparently presupposes a libertarian view of human freedom. This can be defined in the following way: "[G]iven choices A and B, I can literally choose to do either one, no circumstances exist that are sufficient to determine my choice, my choice is up to me, and if I do one of them, I could have attempted to have done otherwise. I act as an agent who is the ultimate originator of at least some of my own actions."[21]

This view of human freedom is extremely controversial; many scholars argue against it. But apparently this outlook is necessary to support the Court's view of personal autonomy, for it is difficult to affirm a person's political autonomy while denying that he or she is metaphysically free to exercise it.

In fact, a libertarian view of human freedom seems best established philosophically by a particular view of the human person, called substance dualism. According to J. P. Moreland, "Substance dualism holds that the brain is a physical substance that has physical properties and the soul is a mental substance that has mental properties. . . . The soul and the brain can interact with each other, but they are different entities with different properties."[22]

Substance dualism is inconsistent, therefore, with views of the human person that deny there exists a real nonphysical thing called a soul or the mind.[23] But if this is the case, the Court must presuppose a particular view of the human person that by definition excludes other views from its consideration.

To illustrate, take abortion. Substance dualism, some have argued, entails the view that a fetus is a human person. Therefore one could argue ironically that the Court cannot justify abortion rights through a claim of personal autonomy without at the same time implicitly passing negative judgment on the abortion rights it seeks to justify and on those views of the human person that deny the existence of a soul.[24]

It seems, then, that when the courts affirm absolute autonomy in the name of neutrality they are not being neutral at all but rather assert or imply a particular view of the human person. This violates their primary reason for their appeal to state neutrality on metaphysical matters.

Thwarting Debate

Justice Kennedy's claim that it is a religious belief to hold that "there is an ethic and morality which transcend human invention" is a disturbing legal doctrine. It thwarts without debate any attempt to challenge either philosophically or legally personal subjective relativism or absolute autonomy. Both views fit well with naturalism, a worldview that denies the existence of anything transcendent.

Kennedy in this statement claims neutrality while committing the law to a particular set of principles. His doctrine establishes philosophical naturalism as the state's official worldview, since it dismisses any ethical position that does not assume naturalism.

The Court could then ignore or dismiss an ethical view that may be more philosophically and constitutionally justified than its rivals merely because it does not presuppose the truth of naturalism.

Could the Court then find unconstitutional the teaching in public schools that immaterial nonnatural entities, such as minds, universals, and numbers, actually exist, since such entities would be transcendent and hence religious? (Would Socrates have to drink the hemlock yet again?) What else would its espousal of philosophical naturalism force it to conclude? Perhaps that human beings are not truly free, since views of the human mind that exclude the existence of an independent soul entail determinism. What then happens to the Fourteenth Amendment's "right to autonomy" if human beings are not truly autonomous? It's like giving a deaf person a "right to hear."

In conclusion, we have seen how in the name of "state neutrality," social philosophers and our legal culture have institutionalized *their* views of social life and the human person. These are hardly neutral but are relativistic, anticommunitarian, and hostile to transcendent views of the human person.

12

Relativism and the Meaning of Marriage

In this chapter and the next we will look at three issues in which the influence of moral relativism is the most pronounced: same-sex marriage, physician-assisted suicide, and abortion.

Questioning and Defending Marriage

The original mission of the homosexual-rights movement called for social tolerance. Now it demands social approval through questioning the state's partiality toward heterosexual monogamy. The movement bases its arguments on the twin dogmas of personal subjective relativism and absolute autonomy, upon which it seeks to build the foundation for same-sex marriage.

Legislation has been passed as a legal attempt to resist this argument. The Defense of Marriage Act (DOMA) was passed in 1996 by the U.S. Congress and was signed by President Bill Clinton. Its purpose is twofold: (1) to allow states not to honor same-sex marriages if such unions are allowed in other states, and (2) to define for the federal code that marriage "means only a legal union between one man and one woman as husband and wife."[1]

For the opponents of same-sex marriage, the passage of DOMA was timely, for it became law soon after the *Romer v. Evans* decision (see chapter 11) and right before a Hawaiian court ruled that forbidding same-sex marriage violated Hawaii's constitution. Incidentally, the judge in the Hawaiian case prohibited the state from distributing marriage licenses to same-sex couples until a higher court makes a ruling.

Consider the comments of two proponents of same-sex marriage on the May 10, 1996, episode of the political talk show *Think Tank*. One of them, Georgetown University law professor William Eskridge, asserts: "[Same-sex marriage is good] primarily for reasons of equality. Legal marriage entails dozens of rights, benefits and obligations which are routinely available to different-sex couples. Those same benefits, rights and obligations should be available on the same terms to lesbian and same-sex couples as a guarantee of their equal rights in our polity."[2]

Echoing these comments is Torie Osborn, former executive director of the National Gay and Lesbian Task Force: "I think it's a question of fundamental fairness. . . . People who are willing to accept the responsibilities of marriage, which is about love, caring, commitment, long-term commitment, should be able to have the right to be married. . . . [D]enying our fundamental humanity is not good for society."[3]

Eskridge and Osborn are calling for the state to remain neutral on the question of marriage; they are saying that the state should not favor any particular marital arrangement. Careful reflection on their position, however, reveals that the state would be far from neutral but rather would be affirming a particular philosophical view of what it means to be a human person in community. To understand this, we need to distinguish between two concepts.

Tolerance or Approval?

How does *social tolerance* differ from *social approval?* How does each concept apply to the question of gay rights? What philosophical presuppositions about the nature of society and its relation to the individual do they carry with them?

Social tolerance asserts that the state should not interfere with the private consensual sex of adults if no one outside the circle of consenters "gets hurt." The state may hold that the behavior is morally wrong and that society ought to discourage it, but because of the impracticality and expense of criminalizing the behavior the state chooses to tolerate it. Proponents of social tolerance need not accept personal subjective relativism and absolute autonomy as fundamental to their political and social philosophy.

The question of social approval is much more complex. It lies at the heart of the debate over same-sex marriage: Should the state be forbidden to give legal and social preference to heterosexual monogamy while denying preference to such alternative lifestyles as homosexuality?

We need to make clear that social tolerance is not the same as social approval. In fact, one can say yes to the privacy rights and call to tolerance implied in the first concept and no to the sexual egalitarianism and social construction theory of human nature or institutions implied in the second.

First, the proponents of same-sex marriage who cling to the concept of social approval assert that sexual activities between consenting adults cannot be judged by objective moral standards as long as the consenters do not include outsiders by coercion and the unions "don't hurt anybody." For it would be unfair to say that one lifestyle is better than another, since there is no objective good—and thus personal subjective relativism is true. Also, a person's choices should be honored regardless of what others may think—and thus absolute autonomy is true. To deny this is to violate "equality."

In this view the state has no right to make judgments about which lifestyle orientation is best and for which the state should provide economic and social incentives. This is sexual egalitarianism.

Second, supporters of same-sex marriage also believe that *all* traditional notions about gender, marriage, and family result from artificial social institutions rather than from an immutable human nature endowed to us by God or nature. This is the social construction theory of human nature and institutions.

Contrast this with what opponents of same-sex marriage believe to be true. They maintain that sexual egalitarianism, the belief that all sexual practices are equal, is false. They hold that informed consent is not a necessary condition for an act to be permissible legally or morally. And they assert that traditional notions of gender, marriage, and family are best understood as the result of moral reflection on human nature and history. However varied these notions have been expressed throughout history, they are part of the furniture of the universe and are essential to maintaining the moral ecology of society.

Problematic Unions

In addition to being nonneutral, the position advocating same-sex marriage is problematic. We will leave the task of a full-blown critique of same-sex marriage and a defense of traditional marriage to others.[4] But we will examine a number of counterintuitive consequences that result from affirming the permissibility of same-sex unions based on the worldview we have described above. Consider just the following.

When traditional marriage is merely a social construction, no principled reason keeps the state from permitting virtually any marital union. For example, marital arrangements that include two brothers, two sisters, a mother and a son, a father and a son, a mother and a daughter, or a grandfather and a grandson, would be consistent with the philosophical assumptions undergirding the same-sex marriage defense.

And this is not all. Nor is a polygamous marriage of one man and numerous spouses—which also may include his mother, his grandmother, his grandfather, as well as his adult daughter and son—inconsistent with the same-sex marriage worldview. Given sexual politics today, one can easily imagine polygamy being reintroduced by an appeal to the sad plight of the bisexual, a person who is incapable of fulfilling his or her marital aspirations with merely *one* spouse of *one* gender. The rhetorical question could be raised: Why should he or she be forbidden from marrying the *ones* he or she loves?

Of course, we cannot ignore the marital rights of the person who has a deep and abiding affection for the family pet, for then the animal-rights crowd may pipe up and accuse us of *speciesism,* the prejudice favoring human beings over nonhuman animals.

To be blunt, the state and its institutions (including public schools) could not say that a heterosexual monogamous couple raising three young children in a traditional Christian, Jewish, or Muslim home is a better arrangement for the moral ecology of the community than the marital union of a father and four of his adult children who make their living producing pornographic films of their sexual encounters. After all, they are all adult consenters, nobody is being coerced, and the state should not prefer one sexual lifestyle over another.

We believe these counterintuitive results occur because most proponents of same-sex marriage presuppose that marriage and family are merely matters of convention and positive law. That is, because family and marital arrangements aren't particularly sacrosanct or normative, individual members of society may tinker with them as long as they don't interfere with other people's choices. The state must be "neutral" and assume no overarching good or purpose to human life, relationships, and communities. Thus those who uphold the philosophy of same-sex marriage must be willing to embrace marital and familial anarchy.

Two Foundations for Marriage

How then should marriage be grounded? In brief, we suggest a two-pronged approach that seems best suited both in preventing counterintuitive results and in grounding traditional marriage: (1) the natural purpose of sexuality and (2) the intrinsic value of traditional marriage.

Man and Woman He Created Them

Opponents of same-sex marriage do not deny that people of the same sex can love each other, but they nevertheless affirm that the purpose of marriage is not *merely* to mark the presence of love. Nor do they argue that the presence of love between persons be thought less of because it does not result in marital union, such as a grandparent's love for a grandchild or a friend's love for another. But as Hadley Arkes points out, "[A] marriage marks something matchless in a framework for the begetting and nurturing of children. In that respect, there is an evident connection between marriage and what has been called the 'natural teleology of the body': namely, the inescapable fact that only two people, not three, only a man and a woman, can procreate a child. It makes a difference, after all, that a child should enter the world in a framework of lawfulness, with parents who are committed to his care for the same reason that they are committed to each other."[5]

This argument has been misunderstood by defenders of same-sex marriage. They argue that since many heterosexual couples are sterile, choose not to have children, or are too old to procreate, therefore it makes no sense to distinguish between heterosexual and same-sex couples because homosexual couples are in the same position as childless heterosexual couples. Or put in the form of a question: Why can't we allow homosexuals to marry each other as we do sterile heterosexual couples, since the homosexuals, like the heterosexuals, are incapable of procreating?[6]

But the argument against same-sex marriage is based on the *nature* of human persons as beings with a gender who have a purpose derived from that nature. That is to say, male human persons are meant for coupling with female human persons, even if their coupling does not result in procreation. This argument is not based on a human person's *function, ability,* or *desire,* which could each be inconsistent with how human persons ought to be by nature.

For example, a person who is comatose, insane, sightless, or sexually desirous of his neighbor's young child lacks something either physically, psychologically, or morally. But he remains a human person who by nature ought to be conscious, sane, seeing, and desiring well. In the same way a sterile, aged, or willingly childless person is still a gendered human person whose purpose for marital union (unless called to celibacy) can only be consummated by one-flesh communion with a spouse of the opposite gender *even if* he or she has contrary desires.

Desires, after all, can be immoral and sometimes harmful to a human person's good, such as desires to overeat, commit adultery, molest children, and engage in gay bashing. Arkes writes:

> But even people who are not covered with college degrees have been able to grasp the natural correspondences that establish the coherence in the design of marriage: There is a natural correspondence between the notion of marriage and the sexual coupling, the merging of bodies, in the "unitive significance" of marriage: and there is the plainest natural connection between that act of coupling and the begetting of children. Those children embody the "wedding" of the couples by combining themselves in the features of both parents.
>
> These meanings are so evident, these natural correspondences so fixed, that nothing in them is impaired if a couple happens to be incapable of begetting children. Their marital acts retain their significance in the unitive scheme of marriage. But if marriage were detached from the "natural teleology of the body," this question may be posed: On what ground of principle could the law confine marriage to "couples"? If the law permitted the marriage of people of the same sex, what is the ground on which the law would refuse to recognize a "marriage" among people who profess that their own love is not confined to a coupling of two, but connected in a larger cluster of three or four? And if that arrangement of plural partners were permitted to people of the same sex, how could it be denied in principle to ensembles of mixed sexes?[7]

Since the purpose of sexuality is derived from our natures as men and women, homosexuals in the strictest sense are no more engaging in sex if they stimulate each other to orgasm than is an ashtray "food" and the act "eating" if one consumes it. This is why Rodney Dangerfield can always elicit a laugh from his audience when he says: "I was afraid the first time I had sex. I was afraid . . . because I was all alone." The audience recognizes that sex alone is not really sex. "It is," comments Arkes, "genital stimulation, but not—as we instantly understand—*really* sex. But in that event, it would not suddenly become 'sex' if two people simply replicated, in tandem, the masturbation implicit in the joke."[8]

Of course, if same-sex proponents simply deny the deriving of certain goods and norms through such a thing as human nature, they undercut the objective basis on which to ground human rights, and more specifically, gay rights. "If natural needs were not the same for all human beings everywhere, at all times and under all circumstances," Mortimer Adler asserts, "we would have no basis for a global doctrine that calls for the protection of human rights by all the nations of the earth."[9]

In other words, *human nature* is a necessary condition for the array of rights, obligations, and virtues many of us take for granted. These rights, however unrecognized, are not contingent upon our wanting, recognizing, or practicing them. Adler goes on to explain, "If all goods were merely apparent, having the aspect of the good only because this or that individual happens to want them, we could not avoid the relativism and subjectivism that would reduce moral judgments to mere opinion. Having no hold on any truth about what is right and wrong, we would be left exposed to the harsh doctrine that might makes right."[10]

Moreover, same-sex–marriage proponents' denial of purpose to the human person equally denies purpose to the human mind, since their worldview asserts that there is no purpose to human nature, which obviously includes the human mind. But when gay-rights activists attack their opponents as being backward or ignorant, they thereby imply that the natural purpose of the human mind is to acquire knowledge and wisdom. After all, if the human person is a socially constructed being with no natural purpose, why should ignorance be wrong if someone desired it and believed herself to be "born that way?"

Thus if the philosophical view of a natural purpose of the body is inadequate to convince proponents of same-sex marriage that their position is incorrect, they must abandon the natural teleology, or purpose, of the mind. The latter view is as well-established philosophically as the former.

An Intrinsic Good

The second foundation for marriage can be best understood when framed in the form of a simple philosophical inquiry: Is marriage more like justice or more like the colors of traffic signals? If it is more like the second and is merely a social convention, then same-sex marriage certainly ought to be permitted. But then, as we have seen, the state would have no principled reason to forbid polygamous, incestuous, or interspecies love-commitments that are attended to by penetration or genital stimulation, just as there is no principled reason why the state should not choose blue, yellow, and pink rather than green, amber, and red as the official traffic signal colors.

If marriage is like justice, however, it has intrinsic value; it is good in itself. The state then cannot morally define marriage in any way it sees fit and call it marriage, just as the state cannot engage in atrocities and by legislative fiat call them justice.

We believe that marriage is more like justice than like the colors of traffic signals. And this is why when marriage is merely a social convention, counterintuitive results occur, such as atrocities becoming "just" because the state says they are.

The intrinsic good of marriage cannot be demonstrated in any strict sense, just as the intrinsic good of justice cannot be demonstrated to the person who insists that a life of ill-gotten gain proves that justice doesn't pay. Professors Robert P. George and Gerard V. Bradley explain:

> . . . [I]f the intrinsic value of marriage, knowledge, [justice], or any other basic human good is to be affirmed, it must be grasped in non-inferential acts of understanding. Such acts require imaginative reflection on data provided by inclination and experience, as well as knowledge of empirical patterns, which underlie possibilities of action and achievement. The practical insight that marriage, for example, has its own intelligible point, and that marriage as a one-flesh communion of persons is consummated and actualized in reproductive-type acts of spouses, cannot be attained by someone who has no idea of what these terms mean; nor can it be attained, except with strenuous efforts of imagination, by people who, due to personal or cultural circumstances, have little acquaintance with actual marriages thus understood. For this reason, we believe that whatever undermines the sound understanding and practice of marriage in a culture—including ideologies hostile to that understanding and practice—makes it difficult for people to grasp the intrinsic value of marriage and marital intercourse.[11]

George and Bradley's point is this: Just as those who are accustomed to seeing injustice pay are not likely to "see" the intrinsic value of justice, so those who are not accustomed to seeing actual marriages will not "see" the point of marriage. The intrinsic value of marriage is grasped through philosophical reflection on human experience, history, and the order of things.

An example of a reflection based on what George and Bradley would call "noninferential acts of understanding" can be found in Harry V. Jaffa's comments: "The family is the foundation of all friendship, as it is the foundation of community . . . the first and most natural of all human associations. . . . Morality comes to sight therefore as the relationship, first of all, of husband and wife, then of parents and children, and of brothers and sisters. From this it expands to include the extended family, the clan, tribe, city, country, and at last mankind. Mankind as a whole is recognized by its generations, like a river which is one and the same while the ever-renewed cycles of death and birth flow on."[12]

Since marriage is an intrinsic good, just as justice is an intrinsic good, a culture that does not nourish, encourage, and protect traditional marriage does so at its own peril. A culture whose institutions do not prize intrinsic value but rather seek justification by appealing to an instrumental value such as desire, want, pleasure, or personal autonomy, harms the souls of its citizens. It deprives them of something of great significance, making it difficult for them to understand why marriage, or anything else, has intrinsic value.

A republican government results from good citizens civilized by such institutions as family, honest work, and good religion. If, to quote Aristotle, statecraft is soulcraft, then the end of the state should be to produce good citizens and therefore provide a privileged position for these institutions. The state should consequently protect traditional marriage in contrast to other alternatives. Since "[m]onogamy, assuming that it is the only valuable form of marriage, cannot be practised by an individual," writes Joseph Raz, "[i]t requires a culture which recognizes it, and which supports it through the public's attitudes and through its formal institutions."[13]

A state that treats all alternative lifestyles as equal, however, does not believe that statecraft is soulcraft and is therefore not particularly interested in producing good citizens qualified to engage in republican government. Rather it is there merely to permit each autonomous individual to decide for himself or herself what is good, true, or beautiful. This state calls itself neutral and "nonjudgmental" when it comes to soulcraft, since all alternatives are equal. This is nihilism with a happy face.

So the debate over same-sex marriage in particular and homosexual rights in general cannot be reduced to a simple dispute between state neutrality and state partiality. Rather it is best described as a culture war between two opposing worldviews. The side that supports same-sex marriage asserts that the state ought to prefer a view of human nature in which human institutions are artificial social constructions ruled by personal subjective preference. The side that supports traditional marriage asserts that the state ought to prefer the view of human nature in which certain human institutions are natural and good and ought to be proffered and encouraged by the state over personal subjective preference.

13

Relativism and the Meaning of Life

As we have seen, our age is filled with disagreement over what have been referred to as "social issues," such as matters of life and death. Unfortunately, many in the general public tend not to deal in a forthright manner with these issues.

For example, instead of trying to answer the question of whether abortion is right or wrong or whether it results in the killing of an innocent human person, some people will simply say it is merely a matter of individual choice. Choice, or one's personal subjective preference, becomes the deciding factor of what is the correct course of action rather than some objective moral standard. This is a form of moral relativism. Although some who support abortion rights are not moral relativists,[1] it seems that an appeal to moral relativism often occurs when the issue is debated in the popular media.

Unrestrained Autonomy in Medicine

Perhaps the most significant contribution of contemporary bioethicists is their affirmation of the principle of respect for autonomy—patient autonomy. The implementation of this principle has empowered patients and moved medicine away from physician paternalism.

But this principle has its problems, which can be—and have been—taken to an extreme.

Dr. Jack Kevorkian and his attorney Geoffrey Fieger have made much of this view in their defense of physician-assisted suicide. Fieger addressed a luncheon at the National Press Club on July 29, 1996, and stated: "I have been at the center of this along with Jack Kevorkian for the last six years, and I am telling you, I have never heard a rational argument why a mentally competent, sick or dying person does not have an absolute right, under certain controlled circumstances, to end their suffering without government. I don't see how rationally you can make an argument in this country, where over 20 years ago, it was declared a fundamental right for a woman to control her own uterus and make decisions about an unborn child."

At the same luncheon, Dr. Kevorkian was much more candid than his attorney in a reply to the moderator, Sonja Hillgren:

> MS. HILLGREN: Many questioners have asked about your religious beliefs. I think you've articulated them, describing yourself as an agnostic. Can you tell us your underlying philosophical belief?
>
> DR. KEVORKIAN: Yeah, it's quite simple: Absolute personal autonomy. I'm an absolute autonomist. Do and say whatever you want to do and say at any time you want to do or say it, as long as you do not harm or threaten anybody else's person or property.

Audience applause followed this exchange. Although Dr. Kevorkian claims to perform physician-assisted suicide on suffering people with terminal illnesses,[2] his application of the principle of autonomy would allow him to practice his specialty on a much larger constituency. In the name of autonomy he could assist in the suicide of the depressed, the downtrodden, and the emotionally vulnerable—or any rational person who wanted to exercise his or her right to absolute autonomy.

This is not to say that Dr. Kevorkian in fact has helped or will help terminate such people. (Some have argued that he has, but this is irrelevant to our critique.) Rather it means that Dr. Kevorkian's lone moral principle justifies such behavior.

Kevorkian and his attorney defend absolute autonomy; they do not promote a more nuanced approach to the question of the ethics of euthanasia. In contrast, some bioethicists believe that physician-assisted suicide in some cases may be morally permissible. These ethicists employ other principles and conclude that in many cases physician-assisted suicide is morally impermissible.[3] The other ethical principles they employ include the principles of beneficence, nonmaleficence, and justice.

In medical ethics the principle of respect for autonomy is a legitimate moral principle. If unrestrained by any other consideration, however, it results in absolute personal autonomy and subjective relativism. And as with same-sex marriage, so too with physician-assisted suicide do these twin principles result in absurd counterintuitive consequences. In short, Kevorkianism is a dangerous and narrow dogma that in the name of tolerance and openness crushes every thoughtful notion or value that its proponents find disagreeable.

A good moral and legal case against physician-assisted suicide has already been made.[4] Our concern here is the misuse of the principle of respect for autonomy by Dr. Kevorkian and his allies.

Terminal Problems

Absolute autonomy in medicine is flawed for many reasons, both legal and moral. Consider the following three.

No Reason Given

The first is that absolute autonomy is based on a dogma for which its proponents typically provide no rationale. Remember Dr. Kevorkian's comments at the National Press Club luncheon: "I'm an absolute autonomist. Do and say whatever you want to do and say at any time you want to do or say it, as long as you do not harm or threaten anybody else's person or property." Many people agree with Kevorkian.

But why are his statements any better than alternative dogmas, such as: "Do and say whatever you want to do and say at any time you want to do or say it, as long as you are consistent with what is morally correct and with living in a community of other people, including your family, neighborhood, and church, synagogue or mosque."

Kevorkian and Fieger may find this alternative too constraining. But if this dogma truly describes reality while Kevorkianism does not, then Kevorkianism puts people in bondage to an autonomy that is wholly unnatural. Human freedom may not be freedom at all if the will is antiseptically amputated from objective moral and social institutions that inform, empower, and nurture personal virtue. Consequently, what Kevorkian and Fieger find as liberating may in fact lead to cold and unnatural solitude. It may deny the patients of the perspective that communal life is much richer than the isolated life of the "unencumbered self."

Recall Fieger's bold confession: "I have never heard a rational argument why a mentally competent, sick or dying person does not have an absolute right, under certain controlled circumstances, to end their suffering without government." And we have yet to hear Fieger and his client's rational argument for absolute, unrestrained, unencumbered personal autonomy. Evidently, Fieger believes that mere assertion justifies his position sufficiently, although he requires his opponents to provide a rationale. Fieger would like us to think otherwise, but Kevorkianism is not the neutral position it pretends to be. It too must be supported by rational argument.

Against Intuition

The second flaw is that Kevorkianism is counterintuitive. To illustrate, consider the following fictional scenario.

Imagine that you are a physician working the emergency room at a large urban hospital. During the night shift three paramedics wheel in an unconscious thirty-three-year-old man who has taken an overdose of barbiturates. Other than his drug overdose, he is in excellent physical condition. You tell your colleagues that he can be saved if his stomach is pumped immediately.

As you are preparing the patient for the procedure, a nurse shows you a note that she found in the young man's pocket. It reads:

> If you find me before I die, please do not pump my stomach. I know exactly what I'm doing. My girlfriend Rebecca has broken up with me and life no longer has any meaning.
>
> I read somewhere that life's meaning and purpose is subjective, so you have no right to judge whether the reason for killing myself is serious or silly. Also, I recently read a book by a Michigan pathologist and during law school the legal briefs of his attorney. They claim that each of us has a right to absolute personal autonomy. During my years in law school I also studied numerous U.S. Supreme Court and federal court decisions. One of them, *Planned Parenthood v. Casey*, says that "at the heart of liberty is the right to define one's own concept of existence, of meaning, of the universe, and of the mystery of human life."
>
> According to my concept of existence, life only has meaning if Rebecca loves me. Rebecca doesn't love me. So life has no meaning *to me*. Now that may seem like a dumb reason for me to kill myself. But I have absolute autonomy to do whatever I want with my body. I choose to kill my body. If you pump my stomach, you violate my autonomy. If I survive, I will sue you for violating my Fourteenth Amendment right to absolute autonomy and to define my own concept of existence, of meaning, of the universe, and of the mystery of human life.

Having read such a note, do you pump the young man's stomach? If you say yes, then your actions convey that such people as physicians may judge which reasons are justifiable for a person to kill himself. Although you may believe that physician-assisted suicide is permissible in some circumstances, the principle of respect for autonomy is not absolute and other considerations must be taken into account.

But if you say no, you must take the counterintuitive position that nothing counts except personal autonomy. You have to assert that medicine as a profession has no purpose other than facilitating the wants of patients, no matter how fanciful or foolish. You must also assert that the individual has no obligations to others, such as family, friends, and community, that should be reflected in law and custom.

In addition, you must hold that family, friends, and community should not be encouraged to consider how the individual's actions, such as committing suicide, affect the moral ecology of such important social institutions as medicine and family. Nor should they weigh the effect on the future generations who will inhabit these institutions; nor should they ponder how such actions may affect the spiritual and moral well-being of the individual who commits them.

In effect, the person who says no to pumping the young man's stomach must admit that no such thing as public and private virtue transcends the desires of the individual. There is no good to which society should strive; human life is not inherently sacred; and no view of human nature is correct if it does not allow for absolute autonomy. Rather there are unencumbered autonomous selves exercising choices in light of their "own concept of existence, of meaning, of the universe, and of the mystery of human life."

Does Suffering End or Begin?

The third flaw is based on Kevorkian's dubious presumption that suicide ends suffering. Mr. Fieger states in his National Press Club speech: "Make no bones about it; we're involved in a fight here. This is not the right to commit suicide. This is not the right to obtain the right to suicide, physician-assisted suicide. It is the right not to suffer."

Don't forget that Dr. Kevorkian is an agnostic when it comes to questions of ultimate concern. Thus he does not deny the existence of God or the afterlife but says that he doesn't know if there is a God or an afterlife. However, according to the major Western religious traditions, including the orthodox versions of Christianity, Islam, and Judaism, those who are not redeemed will be in a place of eternal torment. And according to Dr. Kevorkian, since he is an agnostic, he implicitly concedes there *may be* such a place.

In the Gospel of Matthew (chap. 25), Jesus says this place is reserved for the devil and his angels as well as those Christ never knew, which may include a large percentage of Dr. Kevorkian's patients. If that is the case, then when the doctor assists in their suicides, he may be leading them into greater suffering. And this violates, according to Mr. Fieger, their "right not to suffer."

So, since Dr. Kevorkian is assisting in suicides while admitting he is ignorant of the existence of an afterlife or the spiritual requirements for entering it, it is questionable whether the patients are truly acting autonomously—that is, making free choices with informed consent.

Dr. Jack Kevorkian's appeal to absolute autonomy to justify physician-assisted suicide may currently have support in popular culture and some courts, but his position is fatally flawed. As we have seen, it is not the neutral position its proponents claim. It views the human person as absolutely autonomous, personal subjective relativism as true, and the community as a legal and moral nonentity. In other words, Kevorkianism is partisan. It is grounded in controversial philosophical views about the nature of humanity, morality, and community.

Life or Choice?

Much can be said about the abortion debate and defending the pro-life position.[5] Our purpose, however, is to critique the use of personal subjective relativism and absolute autonomy to inhibit serious debate on the issue. Abortion-rights supporters invoke these principles when they challenge their opponents with one or more of the following arguments: (1) the argument from state neutrality, tolerance, and pluralism, and (2) the argument for neutrality from disagreement over fetal personhood.

Opposing Positions

On January 22, 1997, the twenty-fourth anniversary of *Roe v. Wade* (1973), Vice President Al Gore addressed a gathering sponsored by the National Abortion and Reproductive Rights Action League. He remarked that his position on abortion was not pro-abortion but rather pro-choice; he did not want to say that abortion was good or bad but only that pregnant women should choose for themselves, without government interference.

The vice president's position is quite clear: Those who are pro-choice are neutral and those who are pro-life are partisan. The pro-life position, in other words, violates the twin dogmas of our legal and public culture—personal subjective relativism and absolute autonomy. In short, those who oppose abortion force their moral views on others, hold intolerant views, and are contrary to the American tradition of pluralism.

Because people disagree about abortion, Gore is saying, we ought to permit them to decide for themselves whether abortion is immoral and whether the fetus is a human person. Consequently, if abortion opponents believe that abortion is homicide, they need not fear that the state will coerce them to have an abortion or to participate in the procedure. And on the other side if some people believe that abortion is morally permissible, they need not fear that the state will coerce them to remain pregnant. This, according to conventional wisdom, is the tolerant position one should take in our pluralistic society.

This reasoning may sound nice, but it is *not* neutral. For its proponents fail to grasp why people oppose elective abortion. Perhaps the following examples will make this clear.

During the 1984 presidential campaign the seeming conflict of vice-presidential candidate Geraldine Ferraro's Catholicism with her support of abortion rights was conspicuous in the media. Mario Cuomo, then Governor of New York, gave a speech at the University of Notre Dame and sought to give the tolerance argument intellectual respectability.

His attempt to furnish a philosophical foundation for Ferraro's stance failed. For one cannot appeal to the fact that we live in a pluralistic society, as Cuomo maintained, when the very question of *who* is part of that society is itself the point under dispute. That is, does it or does it not include fetuses? Cuomo lost the argument because he begged the question.

The failure of the tolerance argument can also be illustrated by the actions of the radical antiabortion group Operation Rescue (OR). Its members seek to prevent abortions by disobeying trespassing laws and blocking the entrances of abortion clinics. Regardless of what one thinks about the moral justification of the group's tactics, the members of OR do bring home an undeniable fact: If one believes that fetuses are fully human persons, then the fetuses carried in the wombs of abortion-rights proponents are just as human as those carried in the wombs of those who oppose abortions.

When defenders of the tolerance argument tell opponents of abortion that "pro-lifers have a right to believe what they want to believe about the fetus" and that "they don't have to get abortions if they don't want to," they unwittingly promote the tactics of OR. For abortion opponents believe that a class of persons are being killed by such methods as dismemberment, suffocation, and burning, and thus are more than perplexed to be told that they don't have to participate in the killings if they don't want to. Saying "If you don't like abortion, don't have one" to those opposed to abortion is similar to telling abolitionists not to own slaves if they don't like slavery.

Abortion opponents may be wrong in their view of the fetus and the moral status of abortion. But the tolerance argument does not address this. Consequently, for the defender of the tolerance argument to request that pro-lifers "not force their pro-life belief on others," while simultaneously claiming that "they have a right to believe what they want to believe," is to miss the central point of why most abortion opponents oppose elective abortion.

As we have seen, the tolerance argument is not as neutral as its proponents believe. For to say that women should have the "right to choose" abortions, as abortion-rights proponents proclaim, is tantamount to denying the pro-life position that fetuses are human persons worthy of protection. And to affirm that fetuses are human persons with a "right to life," as abortion opponents proclaim, is tantamount to denying the abortion-rights position that women have a fundamental right to terminate their pregnancies. It seems, then, that the vice president's position is not the neutral one he claims.

What Makes a Person?

In what is arguably the most quoted passage from *Roe v. Wade,* Justice Harry Blackmun, author of the majority opinion, writes: "We need not resolve the difficult question of when life begins. When those trained in the respective disciplines of medicine, philosophy, and theology are unable to arrive at any consensus, the judiciary, at this point in the development of man's knowledge, is not in a position to speculate."[6]

Here Justice Blackmun argues that since experts disagree as to when life begins—when and if the fetus becomes a human person—the Court should not come down on any side. But contrary to his intent, Blackmun fails in his argument to establish government neutrality. When the state leaves the choice of pregnancy termination solely to the individual, it affirms that the fetus is not worthy of state protection and therefore can be discarded without requiring any public justification. Whatever one may think of this public policy, it certainly is not neutral. The Court may have denied taking sides verbally, but the practical effect of its opinion is that the fetus in our society is not a human person worthy of protection.

Imagine you are back in the nineteenth century and the Court is confronted with the issue of enslaving African-Americans. Suppose in the name of state neutrality that it delivers the opinion that it takes no stand on the issue. On that basis it allows white Americans to own blacks as property. The Court may verbally deny taking any position on this issue, but its allowance of slavery is actually morally equivalent to taking a side—that African-Americans are not human persons. Likewise, the Court's verbal denial of taking a position on fetal personhood is contradicted by its conclusion that abortion is a fundamental constitutional right and that fetuses are not persons under the Constitution.

By permitting abortion during the entire nine months of pregnancy,[7] abortion-rights advocates have *decided,* for all practical purposes, when full humanness is attained. They have deemed this moment to occur at birth. Despite their claim that "no one knows when life begins," abortion rights advocates act as if protectable human life begins at birth. Thus, far from being neutral, the Court's opinion in *Roe* affirms a particular perspective on what constitutes a human person.

As we have seen, the notions of personal subjective relativism and absolute autonomy have affected public discussion of such issues as same-sex marriage, physician-assisted suicide, and abortion. Although we believe that in some cases state neutrality is a virtue of good government, it is not a virtue when the government maintains that no objective good exists for which its citizens should aim.

We have also seen that these twin dogmas are not the neutral moral principles that many claim they are in the hope of solving difficult social issues. Rather these people presuppose, or by their application imply, a certain view of what it means to be a human person in community. Clearly a better means for robust discussion and debate must be found.

Part 5

Responding to Relativism

14

Tactics to Refute Relativism

When we reflect carefully on the tenets of relativism and consider the incredibly high price one has to pay to be a consistent relativist, we ask, How could anyone believe this? Who could live this way? The answer is, No one can live this way. People can talk this way, but they can't live this way.

People can wax eloquent in a discussion on moral relativism, but they will complain when someone cuts in front of them in line. They'll object to the unfair treatment they receive at work and denounce injustice in the legal system. They'll criticize crooked politicians who betray the public trust; they will condemn intolerant fundamentalists who force their views on others. Yet these objections are all meaningless in the confused world of moral relativism.

Understanding this inconsistency is the tactical key to proving relativism wrong. The goal is to show that relativism is self-refuting and is such a serious affront to our moral intuition that it is impossible to live it out.

Tactic 1

Show the contradictions of relativism. Ethical relativism is almost always self-refuting in practice. Virtually all relativists fall prey to what Alvin Plantinga of the University of Notre Dame calls a "philosophical tar baby." If relativists try to use certain objections against moralists, they get stuck on their own objections.

Once I was explaining to a waitress in Seattle why I was there attending a theological conference. My comments about religion were all met with an approving nod until I said, "When it comes to religion, people believe a lot of foolish things."[1]

A shadow of disapproval crossed her face. "That's an oppressive view," she said, "not letting people believe what they want to believe."

Much can be said about this remark. For example, notice how to her judging a view foolish was a compromise of liberty, "forcing" my beliefs on others. I ignored that problem, however, and zeroed in on a more fundamental flaw.

"So you're saying I'm wrong, then?"

She balked, not wanting to appear intolerant. "No, I'm just trying to understand your view," she said sweetly.

I couldn't suppress a chuckle. "Be honest; admit it," I said, grinning. "You think I'm wrong."

"No, I don't."

"If you don't think I'm wrong, then why are you correcting me, saying I'm oppressive? And if you think that I am wrong, then why are you 'oppressing' me?"

At a loss for words, she changed the subject.

This conversation exposes a common flaw of relativism. When relativists try to assert their views, they get stuck on Plantinga's tar baby. Comments like "You shouldn't judge others, you intolerant bigot!" show that relativists aren't consistent. They want moral rules to apply to others but not to themselves.

Objections usually take two forms: "You shouldn't force your morality on me" and "Who are you to say?"

"You Shouldn't Force Your Morality on Me"

When confronted with the line, "You shouldn't force your morality on me," simply ask, "Why not?"

This response is effective for two reasons. First, it's only two words; it's simple and easy to remember. Second, it makes the one challenging you justify his objection, putting the ball back in his court where it belongs. He's going to have a hard time explaining why *you* shouldn't impose your views without imposing *his* morality on you. This forces him to state a moral rule while simultaneously denying that moral rules exist.

This same tactic is played out in the following short dialogues:

"You shouldn't force your morality on me."

"Why not?"

"Because I don't believe in forcing morality."

"If you don't believe in it, then by all means, don't do it. Especially don't force *that* moral view of yours on me."

"You shouldn't push your morality on me."

"I'm not entirely sure what you mean by that statement. Do you mean I have no right to an opinion?"

"You have a right to your opinion, but you have no right to force it on anyone."

"Is that your opinion?"

"Yes."

"Then why are you forcing it on me?"

"But you're saying that only *your* view is right."

"Am I wrong?"

"Yes."

"Is that *your* view?

"Yes."

"Then you're saying only *your* view is right, which is the very thing you objected to me saying."

"Don't push your morality on me."

"Why? Don't you believe in morality?"

"Sure, but I believe in *my* morality, not *yours*."

"Well then, how do you know what's moral?"

"I think people should decide individually."

"That's exactly what I'm doing. And I'm deciding *you're* immoral. What's the problem? Live and let live is *your* value, not mine."

"You shouldn't push your morality on me."

"Correct me if I'm misunderstanding you here, but it sounds to me like you're telling me I'm wrong."

"You are."

"Well, you seem to be saying my personal moral view shouldn't apply to other people, but that sounds suspiciously like you are applying your moral view to me. Why are *you* forcing *your* morality on *me?*"

I used this tactic on a relativist who objected when I moralized about his personal choice of homosexuality. "You can't push your morality on me," he charged.

"As a point of information," I responded, "I'm the only one who can even talk about morality in this conversation and make sense, because I believe in an ethical system that allows judgments. You're a relativist, so you can't even say my judgments are wrong."

"Who Are You to Say?"

When someone says, "Who are you to say?" answer with, "Who are you to say 'Who are you to say'?"

You may need to unpack this a little. She's challenging your right to correct another, yet she's correcting you. Your response to her amounts to "Who are you to correct my correction, if correcting in itself is wrong?" or "If I don't have the right to challenge your view, then why do you have the right to challenge mine?" Her objection is self-refuting; you're just pointing it out.

The "Who are you to say?" challenge fails on another count. Taken at face value, the question challenges one's authority to judge another's conduct. It says, in effect, "What authorizes you to make a rule for others? Are you in charge?"

This challenge miscasts my position. I don't expect others to obey me simply because I say so. I'm appealing to reason, not asserting my authority. It's one thing to force beliefs; it's quite another to state those beliefs and make an appeal for them.

The "Who are you to say?" complaint is a cheap shot. At best it's self-defeating. It's an attempt to challenge the legitimacy of your moral judgments, but the statement itself implies a moral judgment.[2]

At worst it legitimizes anarchy. Dennis Prager has accurately pointed out, "Most of the problems with our culture can be summed up in one phrase: 'Who are you to say?'"

Tactic 2

Press their hot button. One of the simplest and most effective ways to refute relativists is to pick their hot button (racism, animal rights, intolerance, gay-bashing, feminism, etc.) and then relativize it. This causes their moral intuition to rise to the surface, undermining their position.

A seventeen-year-old high school student told me he'd been talking to a teacher who claimed that all morality is relative.

"How do I refute her?" he asked.

"Steal her stereo," I said. "In situations like this," I explained, "you'll learn more by her reactions than by her arguments."

A belief is a propensity to act as if a thing were true. Our actions—and, in some cases, our reactions—are a guide to our true beliefs. A relativist's natural response when evil strikes close to home will usually betray her. She says she rejects morality, but in reality she still believes in it. Her actions tell the true story.

Betrayed by Words

Our language is another key that reveals what we really believe. It's virtually impossible for relativists to talk in a way that is consistent with their beliefs. The words we use bear testimony to our deepest intuitions about the world.

If you encounter someone who thinks he's a relativist, you can usually prove him wrong in five minutes when moral words like *should* creep into the conversation. When they do, expose the inconsistency.

This tactic works for a good reason: Morality is built in. Human beings have an innate capacity to reason in moral categories and to make accurate moral judgments.

This is where intuition plays an important role. Instead of arguing for morality, we ask a question or make a comment that gets the person in touch with her own moral intuition. We then ask her to make sense out of her response in light of her relativism.

What's Wrong with Judging?

The power of this approach is illustrated in my conversation with a physical therapist I'll call Bill.

Bill was a friendly, tolerant sort, willing to talk with me about Christianity until the question of homosexuality came up. My apparent lack of tolerance made him uncomfortable, and he said so.

"That's what bugs me about Christians," he said. "You seem nice at first, but then you start getting judgmental."

"What's wrong with that?" I said. It was a leading question.

"It's not right to judge other people."

"If it's wrong to judge people, Bill, then why are you judging me?"

This question stopped him in his tracks. He'd been impaled on his own principle, and he knew it.

"You're right," he admitted. "I was judging you. Kind of hard to avoid it." He paused a moment, scratched his head, and regrouped.

"How about this? It's okay to judge people, as long as you don't force *your* morality on *them*," he said, thinking he was on safer ground. "That's when you cross the line."

"Okay, Bill, can I ask you a question?"

"Sure."

"Is that *your* morality?"

"Yes."

"Then why are you pushing your morality on *me?*" Bill was getting stuck on Plantinga's tar baby.

He tried a couple more false starts but couldn't extract himself. Finally in frustration he said, "This isn't fair!"

"Why not?" I asked.

"I can't find a way to say it so it sounds right." He thought I was playing a word trick on him.

"Bill, it doesn't *sound* right because it *isn't* right; it's self-refuting," I explained.

At this point in the conversation some people throw up their hands and say, "Now you've got me confused."

In these cases I respond, "No, you were confused when you started. You just now realized it."

Tactic 3

Force the tolerance issue. The third tactic makes capital of a relativist's commitment to tolerance.

Many people are confused about what tolerance is. According to *Webster's New World Dictionary, Second College Edition,* tolerance means to allow or to permit, to recognize and respect others' beliefs and practices without sharing them, to bear or put up with someone or something not necessarily liked.

Tolerance, then, involves permitting or allowing a conduct or point of view you think is wrong while respecting the person in the process.

Notice that we can't tolerate others unless we disagree with them. We don't "tolerate" people who share our views. Instead tolerance is reserved for those we think are wrong.

This essential element of tolerance—disagreement—has been completely lost in the modern distortion of the concept. Nowadays, if you think someone is wrong, you're called intolerant.

This presents us with a curious problem. Judging someone as wrong makes one intolerant, yet one must first think another is wrong in order to be tolerant. It's a catch-22. According to this approach, true tolerance is impossible.

Adding to the confusion is the fact that tolerance could apply to persons, behaviors, or ideas.

The classical definition of tolerance, what might be called "civic tolerance," can be equated with the word *respect.* We respect people who hold beliefs different than our own; we treat them courteously and allow their views in the public discourse, even though we may strongly disagree with them and vigorously contend against their ideas in the public square.

Note that respect is accorded to the *person* here. Whether his or her *behaviors* should be tolerated, however, is a different issue. This is the second sense of tolerance. Our laws demonstrate that people may believe what they like—and they usually have the liberty to express those beliefs—but they may not behave as they like. Some behavior is immoral and a threat to the common good and so is not tolerated but restricted by law.

Tolerating people should also be distinguished from tolerating ideas. Civic tolerance says that all views should get a courteous hearing, not that all views have equal worth, merit, or truth. The view that no person's ideas are any better or truer than those of another is irrational and absurd. To argue that some views are false, immoral, or just plain silly does not violate any meaningful standard of tolerance.

These three categories are frequently conflated by muddled thinkers. If we reject another's *idea* or *behavior,* we're automatically accused of rejecting the *person* and of being disrespectful. To say we're intolerant of the *person* because we disagree with her *idea* is confused. On this view of tolerance, no idea or behavior can be opposed, regardless of how graciously, without inviting the charge of incivility.

Historically, our culture has usually emphasized tolerance of all persons but not tolerance of all behavior. This is a critical distinction because, in the current rhetoric of relativism, the concept of tolerance is most frequently advocated for behavior—premarital sex, abortion, homosexuality, pornography, and so on.

Ironically, though, there is little tolerance for the expression of contrary *ideas* on issues of morality and religion. Differing views are soundly censured. The tolerance issue has thus gone topsy-turvy: Tolerate most behavior, but don't tolerate opposing beliefs about those behaviors. Contrary moral opinions are labeled as "imposing your view on others."

Instead of hearing, "I respect your view," those who differ in certain ways are deemed bigoted, narrow-minded, and intolerant.

Most of what passes for tolerance today is not tolerance at all but actually intellectual cowardice. Those who hide behind that word are often afraid of intelligent engagement and don't engage or even consider contrary opinions. It's easier to hurl an insult than to confront the idea and either refute it or be changed by it.

The classical rule of tolerance is still a good guideline: Tolerate persons in all circumstances by according them respect and courtesy. Tolerate (allow) behavior that is moral and consistent with the common good, and tolerate (accept) ideas that are sound.

Tactic 4

Have a ready defense. Taking the offensive is a key strategy when dealing with relativism. You'll have to answer some questions in the process, though, so be ready. Here are a few common rejoinders and some defensive maneuvers to use in reply.

Whose Values?

One of the most common responses to a critique of relativism is, "Whose values are right?"

In our experience, this may sound like a valid refutation of morality, but it's not. Rather it's a sophisticated dismissal of the issue. The inference is that since true absolutes may be difficult to distinguish, absolutes don't exist.

This mixes two distinct questions about absolutes: the ontological question—Do moral absolutes exist?—and the epistemological question—How do we know what they are? These categories should be kept separate, however. Constructing a full classification of moral rules to live by is difficult, but foundational principles are obvious and only one is needed to prove the case against moral relativism.

Louis Pojman poses the question, "So who's to judge what's right or wrong?" and answers, "We are. We are to do so on the basis of the best reasoning we can bring forth and with sympathy and understanding."[3] He adds: "We can reason and perform thought experiments in order to make a case for one system over another. We may not be able to know with certainty that our moral beliefs are closer to the truth than those of another culture or those of others within our own culture, but we may be justified in believing that they are. If we can be closer to the truth regarding factual or scientific matters, why can't we be closer to the truth on moral matter?"[4]

The next objection is a variation of the first.

What Are They?

A favorite ploy of professors whose relativism is challenged by students in their class is to respond, "Oh, you believe in absolutes?

What are they?" When these professors raise the second issue, asking what the absolutes are, they think they have refuted the students on the first. In reality, all they've succeeded to do is change the topic.

When instructors make a case for relativism in class, it's entirely appropriate to challenge them by citing the flaws listed in earlier chapters. When they promote ethical subjectivism based on cultural relativism, ask, "How does it follow that if people have different points of view, then nobody's right?" As we saw earlier, this is the error of Society Does Relativism.

But what do we say when a professor asks, "If you believe in moral absolutes, what are they?" We might offer that it's immoral to dock the pay of professors just because they are Jewish, or African-American, or women, or approve of homosexuals, or whatever the current hot button happens to be.

Chances are, though, if we suggest a moral absolute, they'll cite those who disagree. They may think they have made their case, but their reasoning is circular. They're only repeating the error we're challenging. It doesn't follow that if people disagree, then morals are relative.

Both of these responses, though legitimate, miss the real point: The professor has changed the subject. She challenges us to defend our view, but we haven't expressed a view. She, however, is making a specific claim about morality and is sidestepping the challenge. The burden of proof is on her.

We offer one possible response: "Professor, it doesn't really matter what I believe. I'm not making the claim. *You* are. I may even believe as you do, for all you know. I'm just asking you to prove your point.

"I asked a fair question and you changed the subject, throwing it back on me. I'm not making any claim about morality. But you're teaching that morality is relative because you think cultures have different values. I'm simply asking if that works. So please tell me how your conclusion follows."

Students should not be afraid to challenge their professors if they do so with grace and respect.

We may have good reason to believe that moral absolutes exist, even though we may not be able to list every one. All that's needed is one clear-case example. And when challenged, professors will usually provide it themselves if their hot-button issue is hit.

Problems with Intuition

Objections to moral intuition usually take two forms.

First, some relativists deny the existence of plain moral facts. They're willing—at least in discussion—to disavow the objective validity of such things as genuine evil, justice, fairness, honesty, tolerance, moral improvement, and the like.

Frankly, we don't believe them. As we showed earlier, sooner or later their conduct, reactions, or language will give them away. Spend a day with them, and dozens of examples that belie their apparent commitment to moral relativism will surface.

What do they teach their children? Remember, our actions betray our true beliefs. Every time relativists speak or act in a way that implies a moral judgment, expresses a moral rule, or provides moral education, they violate their own view.

But if relativists are consistent, there's another problem: Those who deny all morality are twisted and a threat to society. On their view, the worst that could be said of Charles Manson is that he had a bad-hair day or of Jeffrey Dahmer that he had an eating disorder.

Simply denying morality is not good enough. One needs to offer some compelling reason why rape, torturing a newborn child for pleasure, or punishing an innocent person are morally benign. The burden of proof is on the one who denies plain moral truth.

Relativists can't win. If they deny moral intuition, they are either lying, fooling themselves, or are sick and need help.

A second approach some take is to offer a competing set of moral "intuitions." I have mine; they have theirs. Therefore morals are relative. This is the same worn-out fallacy of Society Does Relativism trying to lift its head again. As we have seen, differences do not prove that no one is correct.

Further, it's always fair to ask, "In what way is your appeal to intuition the same kind of appeal as mine?" Just calling something an intuition doesn't necessarily make it one. It's easy to say, "You're wrong." But it's much harder to show why.

For example, if you dispute our case for moral common sense by citing some parochial practice among hill-tribe peoples in southeast Asia that "makes sense" to them, we're going to want to know why we should consider that a genuine intuition and not just a tribal custom.

We give clear-case examples (like it's wrong to punish an innocent person because he's innocent) for a reason. Each of the things we've mentioned has a universal quality and leads to a careful justification of our view. Any contrary claim requires the same if it's to be taken seriously.

The Bankruptcy of Relativism

Relativism is bankrupt. It's not a true moral system. It's self-refuting. It's undermined by serious counterexamples. It makes morality unintelligible. It's not even tolerant.

When Tolerance Makes Sense

The principle of tolerance doesn't follow logically from any form of relativism. Society Does Relativism (descriptive relativism) tells us only about culture; it says nothing about morality. No valid moral principle can be deduced from the observation that cultures seem to differ in their moral viewpoints. If from this we conclude that morality is relative, then we certainly can't impose the objective moral rule of tolerance on other cultures.

Society Says Relativism (normative relativism) dictates that one ought to follow the moral rules of one's own culture. Even here, though, tolerance is required only if one's particular society values it. Many don't. If a culture values intolerance, then its citizens are obliged to be intolerant. As a principle, tolerance has no independent moral force of its own. Further, one culture can't impose its view of tolerance on another.

In I Say Relativism (individual ethical relativism) morality is purely an individual matter. Since by definition moral truth is relative to a person's private convictions, it is inappropriate to prescribe universal statements like "All people ought to be tolerant of others' viewpoints."

The principle of tolerance makes sense only in a world in which moral absolutes exist, and only if one of those absolutes is "All people should respect others' rights to differ."

The ethic of tolerance can be rational only if moral truth is objective and absolute, not subjective and relative. Tolerance is an absolutist principle and makes no sense from any view of ethical relativism.[5]

The Consequences of Relativism

People are drowning in a sea of moral relativism. Relativism destroys the conscience. It produces people without scruples, because it provides no moral impulse to improve. This is why we don't teach relativism to our children. In fact, we labor to teach them just the opposite.

Ultimately relativism is self-centered and egoistic. "Doing our own thing" is fine for us, but we don't want others to be relativists. We expect them to treat us decently.

Relativism is also dangerous. At Auschwitz, Hitler declared, "I freed Germany from the stupid and degrading fallacies of conscience and morality. . . . We will train young people before whom the world will tremble."[6]

Regarding morality, we are faced with only two possibilities: either morality or nonmorality, either moral objectivism or moral relativism. There are no other choices.

Morality is either objective, and therefore absolute in some sense and universal, or not objective, and therefore personal and subjective, mere opinion. These are the only choices. If moral relativism is bankrupt, as we've demonstrated, then some form of moral absolutism must be true.

Morals exist. There's no way around it. This conclusion has radical consequences for the way we see the world.

15

Monkey Morality

Given that objective moral rules exist, we face other questions: What is the best explanation for moral rules? In what kind of world does morality make sense? In short, Why morality?

When we ask these questions, an increasingly popular answer has been given: evolution. In this chapter we will explore whether Darwinism can account for the existence of moral principles.

Gene-Based Feelings?

One of the strongest evidences for the existence of God is the unique human moral nature. C. S. Lewis argues in *Mere Christianity* that a persistent moral law represents the ethical foundation of all human cultures. This, he says, is evidence for the God who created the moral law.

But not everyone agrees. Some claim that rudimentary forms of morality exist among animals, especially the "higher" primates like chimpanzees. They therefore suggest that morality in humans is not unique and can be explained by the natural process of evolution without appeal to a divine lawgiver.

This view of morality is one of the conclusions of the new science of evolutionary psychology. Its adherents advance a simple premise: The mind, just like every part of the physical body, is a product of evolution. Everything about human personality—marital relationships, parental love, friendships, dynamics among siblings, social climbing, and even office politics—can be explained by the forces of neo-Darwinian evolution.

Advocates of this new view would claim that even the moral threads that make up the fabric of society are the product of natural selection. Thus morality can be reduced to chemical relationships in the genes based on different evolutionary needs in the physical environment. Love and hate, guilt and remorse, gratitude and envy, and even the virtues of kindness, faithfulness, or self-control can all be explained mechanistically through the cause and effect of chance genetic mutations and natural selection.

One notable example of this challenge to the transcendent nature of morality comes from the book written by journalist Robert Wright, *The Moral Animal—Why We Are the Way We Are: The New Science of Evolutionary Psychology.*

Evolving Morals

The Blind Moral-Maker

In his popular defense of evolution, *The Blind Watchmaker,* Oxford zoologist Richard Dawkins acknowledges that although the biological world looks designed, this appearance is deceiving. The appearance of intelligent order actually results from the workings of natural selection.

Robert Wright holds the same view regarding humanity's psychological features, including morality. His argument rests on the nature of natural selection itself: "If within a species there is variation among individuals in their hereditary traits, and some traits are more conducive to survival and reproduction than others, then those traits will (obviously) become more widespread within the population. The result (obviously) is that the species' aggregate pool of hereditary traits changes."[1]

Wright argues from effect back to cause, asking what best explains the results we see. To Wright, the evolutionary explanation is obvious. To survive, animals must adapt to changing conditions. Through the process of natural selection, naturalistic forces "choose" certain behavior patterns that allow the species to continue to exist. We call those patterns morality.

Wired for Morality

The thesis that evolution explains all moral conduct requires such conduct to be determined by the genes. Wright sees a genetic connection with a whole range of emotional capabilities. He talks about "genes inclining a male to love his offspring"[2] and romantic love that was not only invented by evolution but corrupted by it.[3] Consider these comments:

> If a woman's "fidelity gene" (or her "infidelity gene") shapes her behavior in a way that helps get copies of *itself* into future generations in large numbers, then that gene will by definition flourish [emphasis in the original].[4]

> Beneath all the thoughts and feelings and temperamental differences that marriage counselors spend their time sensitively assessing are the stratagems of the genes—cold, hard equations composed of simple variables.[5]

Some mothers have a genetic predisposition to love their children, so the story goes, and this predisposition is favored by natural selection. Consequently, more women are good mothers.

What is the evidence, though, that moral virtues are genetic, a random combination of molecules? Is the fundamental difference between a Mother Teresa and a Hitler their chromosomal makeup? If so, then how could we ever praise Mother Teresa? Or how could a man like Adolf Hitler be truly guilty?

Wright, however, offers no such empirical evidence. He assumes that moral qualities are in the genes because he must; his paradigm would fail otherwise.

Wright's Double-Standard

Morality above Morality

In a promotional piece for his book, Wright says, "My hope is that people will use the knowledge [in this book] not only to improve their lives—as a source of 'self-help'—but as cause to treat other people *more decently*" (emphasis ours).

This statement captures a major flaw in Wright's analysis. His entire thesis is that chance evolution explains morality, that the environment selects those whose morals are beneficial for survival. Morality is a product of nature.

Yet Wright frequently lapses, unconsciously making reference to a morality that seems to transcend nature. Take this comment: "Human beings are a species splendid in their array of moral equipment, *tragic* in their propensity to *misuse* it, and *pathetic* in their constitutional ignorance of the *misuse*" (emphasis ours).[6] Wright reflects on the moral equipment randomly given to us by nature and then bemoans our immoral use of it with such words as *tragic, pathetic,* and *misuse.*

He writes, "Go above and beyond the call of a smoothly functioning conscience; help those who aren't likely to help you in return, and do so when nobody's watching. This is one way to be a truly moral animal."[7]

It's almost as if he has two categories of morality—nature's morality and a transcendent standard used to judge nature's morality. But where did this transcendent standard come from? If transcendent morality judges the "morality" that evolution is responsible for, then it can't itself be accounted for by evolution.

Social Darwinism

Like many evolutionists, Wright recoils from social Darwinism, in which the principle of survival of the fittest is applied to society. Just because nature exploits the weak, he argues, doesn't mean we are morally obliged to do so. "Natural selection's indifference to the suffering of the weak is not something we need to emulate. Nor should we care whether murder, robbery, and rape are in some sense 'natural.' It is for us to decide how abhorrent we find such things and how hard we want to fight them."[8]

Wright argues that life in an unregulated state of nature is "solitary, poor, nasty, brutish, and short,"[9] in seventeenth-century English philosopher Thomas Hobbes's words, but that we're not required to take the "survival of the fittest" as a moral guideline.

Evolutionists may be right when they say that we're not compelled to adopt the morality of evolution. The danger of social Darwinism, however, is not that society must adopt the law of the jungle but rather that it is allowed to. The exploitation of the weak by the strong is morally benign according to Wright's evolutionary view of morality.

What Darwinists cannot do is give us a reason why we ought not simply copy nature and destroy those who are weak, unpleasant, costly, or just plain boring. If all moral options are legitimate, then it's acceptable for the strong to rule the weak. No moral restraints would protect the feeble, because moral restraints simply wouldn't exist.

A Chimp's Conduct

Recent studies have attempted to show that animals exhibit rudimentary moral behavior. In one case, a group of chimpanzees "punished" Bongo, a "selfish" member of their band, by withholding food from him. Apparently the moral rule was this: Chimps shouldn't be selfish.

Conduct, Motive, and Intent

This assessment has serious problems. First, drawing conclusions about animal morality simply from external behavior reduces morality to conduct. But true morality also entails nonbehavioral elements, too, like intent and motive.

We can't infer actual moral obligations from the mere fact of a chimp's conduct. We can observe that chimps in community share food and that when they do they survive better. But we can't conclude from this that Bongo *ought* to share his bananas or else he'll be immoral because he hasn't contributed to the survival of his community.

Further, in fixing blame we distinguish between an act done by accident and the same act committed on purpose. The behavior is the same, but the intent is different. We don't usually blame people for accidents: If the boy didn't intend to trip the old lady, we don't fault him.

We also give attention to the issue of motive. We withhold blame even if the youngster tripped the elderly woman on purpose if the motive is acceptable: He tripped her to keep her from running in front of a train. Hadley Arkes makes this distinction clearly: "Whether the taking of property was a theft or a borrowing turned on the understanding that animated the actors. It was entirely possible that the outward acts, in two separate cases, could be virtually identical—e.g., someone went to a garage and took a hose—but the two events might have an entirely different moral significance, and they would lead to moral judgments that were markedly different."[10]

Motive and intent cannot be determined simply by looking at behavior. In fact, some good behavior might turn out to be tainted, depending on the motive and intent: giving to the poor when one wants to be well thought of, instead of having a genuine concern for the recipients. Indeed, it seems one can be immoral without any behavior at all, such as plotting an evil deed that one is never able to carry out.

Morality informs behavior, judging it either good or bad; it's not identical to behavior. Rather it is something deeper than habitual patterns of physical interaction. Therefore we can't draw conclusions about animal morality simply based on what we observe in their conduct.

Morality: Explained or Denied?

This leads us to the second problem, which runs much deeper than the first. When morality is reduced to patterns of behavior chosen by natural selection for the survival value, then morality is not explained; it's denied. Wright admits as much. Regarding the conscience he says: "The conscience doesn't make us feel bad the way hunger feels bad, or good the way sex feels good. It makes us feel as if we have done something that's wrong or something that's right. Guilty or not guilty. It is amazing that a process as amoral and crassly pragmatic as natural selection could design a mental organ that makes us feel *as if* we're in touch with higher truth. Truly a shameless ploy" (emphasis ours).[11]

Evolutionists like Wright are ultimately forced to admit that what we think is a "higher truth" of morality turns out to be a "shameless ploy" of nature, a description of animal behavior conditioned by the environment for survival. We've given that conduct a label, they argue: morality. But they say there is no real right and wrong.

Does Bongo, the chimp, actually exhibit genuine moral behavior? Does he understand the difference between right and wrong? Does he make principled choices to do what's right? Is he worthy of blame and punishment for doing wrong? Of course not, Wright says. Bongo merely does in a primitive way what humans do in a more sophisticated manner. We respond according to our genetic conditioning, a program "designed" by millions of years of evolution.

Philosopher Michael Ruse admits that evolution and objective morality are at odds: "Considered as a rationally justifiable set of claims about an objective something, ethics is illusory. I appreciate that when somebody says, 'Love thy neighbor as thyself,' they think they are referring above and beyond themselves. . . . Never the less . . . such reference is truly without foundation. Morality is just an aid to survival and reproduction . . . and any deeper meaning is illusory."[12]

The evolutionary approach does not explain morality; it denies it. Instead, it explains why we think moral truths exist when, in fact, they don't.

Why Be Good Tomorrow?

This third observation uncovers the third and most serious objection to the idea that evolution is adequate to explain morality. One question can never be answered by any evolutionary assessment of ethics: Why ought I be moral tomorrow?

One of the distinctives of morality is its "oughtness," its moral incumbency. Assessments of mere behavior, however, are descriptive only. Since morality is essentially prescriptive—telling what *should* be the case as opposed to what *is* the case—and since all evolutionary assessments of moral behavior are descriptive, then evolution cannot account for the most important thing that needs to be explained: morality's "oughtness."

One question really needs to be answered: Why shouldn't the chimp (or a human, for that matter) be selfish? The evolutionary answer might be that when we're selfish, we hurt the group. That answer, however, presumes another moral value, that we ought to be concerned about the welfare of the group. But why should that concern us? They would say because if the group doesn't survive, then the species doesn't survive. But why should we care about the survival of the species?

Here's the problem. The responses intended to explain morality ultimately depend on some prior moral notion to hold them together. Based on an evolutionary view, it is difficult to explain why we should not be selfish, or steal, or rape, or even kill tomorrow without smuggling morality into the answer.

The evolutionary explanation disembowels morality, reducing it to mere descriptions of conduct. The best the Darwinist explanation can do—if it succeeds at all—is explain *past* behavior. It cannot inform future actions. But prescription, not description, is the essence of morality. As we have seen, evolution may be one explanation for the existence of conduct we choose to call moral, but it gives no reason why we should obey any moral rules in the future. If one countered that we have a moral obligation to evolve, then I've won my point. If we have moral obligations prior to evolution, then evolution itself can't be their source.

Evolutionists Are Wrong about Ethics

Darwinists opt for an evolutionary explanation for morality without sufficient justification. To make their naturalistic explanation work, morality must reside in the genes. Good and beneficial tendencies can then be chosen by natural selection. Nature, through the mechanics of genetic chemistry, cultivates behaviors we call morality.

As we have seen, this creates two problems. First, evolution doesn't explain what it's meant to explain. It can only account for preprogrammed behavior, not moral choices. Moral choices, by their nature, are made by free agents. They are not determined by internal mechanics.

Second, the Darwinist explanation reduces morality to mere descriptions of behavior. The morality that evolution needs to account for, however, entails much more than conduct. Minimally, it involves motive and intent as well. Both are nonphysical elements that can't, even in principle, evolve in a Darwinian sense.

Further, this assessment of morality, being descriptive only, ignores the most important moral question of all: Why should I be moral *tomorrow?* Evolution cannot answer that question. Morality dictates what future behavior ought to be. Darwinism can only attempt to describe why humans acted in a certain way in the past.

Evolution does not explain morality. Bongo is not a bad chimp; he's just a chimp. No moral rules apply to him. Eat the banana, Bongo.

16

Why Morality?

Where do morals come from? Why do they seem to apply only to human beings? Are they the product of chance? What worldview makes sense out of morality? As we asked earlier, Why morality?

We can answer these questions simply by reflecting on the nature of moral rules. By making observations about the effect—morality—we can then ask what are its characteristics and what might cause it.

Four Observations

The first thing we observe about moral rules is that although they exist, they are not physical, because they don't have physical properties. We won't bump into them in the dark. They don't extend into space. They have no weight. They have no chemical characteristics. Instead they are immaterial things we discover not through the aid of our five senses but by the process of thought, introspection, and reflection.

This is a profound realization. We have, with a high degree of certainty, stumbled upon something real. Yet it's something that can't be proven empirically or described in terms of scientific laws. From this we learn that there's more to the world than just the physical universe. If nonphysical things—like moral rules—truly exist, then materialism as a worldview is false.

Many other things seem to populate this invisible world, such as propositions, numbers, and the laws of logic. Values like happiness, friendship, and faithfulness exist, too, along with meanings and language. There may even be persons—souls, angels, and other divine beings.

Our discovery also tells us that some things really exist that science has no access to, even in principle. Some things are not governed by scientific laws. Science, therefore, is not the only discipline that gives us true information about the world. It follows, then, that naturalism as a worldview is also false.

To deny either of these conclusions, one must repudiate the existence of objective moral rules and also answer the difficulties of relativism raised in the previous chapters.

Our discovery of moral rules forces us to expand our understanding of the nature of reality and open our minds to the existence of a host of new things that populate the world in the invisible realm.

The second thing we observe is that moral rules are a kind of communication. They are propositions—intelligent statements of meaning conveyed from one mind to another. The propositions take the form of imperatives, or commands. A command only makes sense when there are two minds involved, one giving the command and one receiving it.

We notice a third thing when we reflect on moral rules. They have a force we can actually feel *prior* to any behavior. This is called the incumbency of moral rules, the "oughtness" of morality we discussed earlier. It appeals to our will, compelling us to act in a certain way, though we may disregard its force and choose not to obey.[1]

Fourth and finally, we feel a deep discomfort when we violate clear and weighty moral rules; an ethical pain makes us aware that we have done something wrong and deserve punishment. This sense of guilt carries with it not just this uncomfortable awareness but also the dread of having to answer for our deed. Distraction and denial may temporarily numb the pain, but it never disappears entirely.

Narrowing Our Options

These four observations provide us with a foundation from which to answer the question, Why morality? We need only determine the possible options and then ask which option best accounts for our observations.

A word of caution here. At this point our discussion becomes personal because the ultimate answer to our question has serious ramifications for the way we live our lives. We may be tempted to abandon careful thinking when we are forced to confront conclusions that make us uncomfortable. Faced with a limited number of options, we must choose something. When the full range of choices is clear, rejection of one means acceptance of another.

Our options are limited to three. One: Morality is simply an illusion. Two: Moral rules exist but are mere accidents, the product of chance. Three: Moral rules are not accidents but are the product of intelligence. Which option makes most sense given our four observations about morality?

Some argue that morals simply don't exist. They are nothing but illusions, useful fictions that help us live in harmony. This, as we have seen, is the relativist's answer we found seriously wanting when we discussed this option in chapter 7.

Some take a second route. They admit that although objective moral laws must exist, they are just accidents. We discover them as part of the furniture of the universe, so to speak, but they have no explanation, nor do we need one.

This won't do for a good reason: Moral rules without grounds or justification need not be obeyed. An example may help to illustrate: One evening in the middle of a Scrabble game, you notice the phrase "do not go" formed in the random spray of letter tiles on the table. Is this a command that ought to be obeyed? Of course not. It's just a random collection of letters.

Commands are communications between two minds. Chance might conceivably create the appearance of a moral rule, but there can be no command if no one is speaking. Since this phrase is accidental, it can be safely ignored.

Even if a person is behind the communication, one could ignore the command if it isn't backed by an appropriate authority. If I stood at an intersection and put my hand up, cars might stop voluntarily, but they'd have no duty to respond. They could ignore me without fear of punishment because I have no authority to direct traffic. But if a police officer replaced me, traffic would come to a halt.

What is the difference between the officer and me? My authority is not grounded. It doesn't rest on anything solid. Police, in contrast, represent the government, so their authority is justified. They are legitimate representatives the state appoints to carry out its will.

Thus a law has moral force when an appropriate authority, operating within its legitimate jurisdiction, issues it. If people violate such a law, they could be punished. The same is true of moral laws. These laws have force if a proper authority stands behind them. Moral rules that appear by chance, in contrast, have no such grounding.

Our second option fails because it doesn't explain three of the important features we observed about morality. Chance morality fails to be a communication between two minds and therefore cannot be imperative. It doesn't account for the incumbency of moral rules nor does it make sense of the guilt and expectation of punishment one feels when those rules are violated.

Only one answer remains as a possible source of morality. If morality is neither an illusion nor the product of chance, then morals must be the result of an intelligent designer. Universal moral laws that have genuine incumbency require an author whose proper domain is the universe, who has the moral authority to enforce his laws and the power ultimately to mete out perfect justice.

What best explains the existence of morality? A personal God whose character provides an absolute standard of goodness. An impersonal force won't do because a moral rule encompasses both a proposition and a command; both are features of minds. Ethicist Richard Taylor explains: "A duty is something that is owed . . . but something can be owed only to some person or persons. There can be no such thing as a duty in isolation. . . . The concept of moral obligation [is] unintelligible apart from the idea of God. The words remain, but their meaning is gone."[2]

Only one option makes sense of each observation about morality: a personal God who created both the material and the immaterial domain. Moral laws suggest a moral law-giver, one who communicates his desires through his laws. He expects his imperatives to be obeyed.

The existence of God also explains the incumbency of morality. Ethics are adequately grounded because God is a proper authority for moral rules. The universe is his possession because he created it; he has the right to rule over it.

Ethical pain—true moral guilt—also makes sense with this explanation. Morals are not disembodied principles but personal commands, and so a violation is not just a broken rule but an offense against the person who made the rule. Danish philosopher Søren Kierkegaard pointed out that a person could not have anything on his conscience if God did not exist.

Some attempt to argue that they don't need God to have morality. They can live a moral life even though they don't believe in a divine being. But no one argues that an atheist can't behave in a way one might call moral. The real question is, Why ought he? Trappist monk Thomas Merton put it this way: "In the name of whom or what do you ask me to behave? Why should I go to the inconvenience of denying myself the satisfactions I desire in the name of some standard that exists only in your imagination? Why should I worship the fictions that you have imposed on me in the name of nothing?"[3]

A moral atheist is like someone sitting down to dinner who doesn't believe in farmers, ranchers, fishermen, or cooks. She believes the food just appears, with no explanation and no sufficient cause. This is silly. Either her meal is an illusion or someone provided it. In the same way, if morals really exist, as we have argued, then some cause adequate to explain the effect must account for them. God is the most reasonable solution.

The Final Verdict

The defeat of relativism makes certain conclusions unavoidable. If relativism is false, some form of moral objectivism must be true. Morals therefore exist. We need not give a complete outline of ethical guidelines to make our case. If even one moral absolute exists, it invites the question, What kind of worldview explains this moral rule?

Atheism can't make any sense of it. Neither can most Eastern religions. If reality is an illusion, as they hold, then the distinction between good and evil is ultimately rendered meaningless. Something like the Judeo-Christian or Muslim idea of God must be true to account for moral laws adequately.[4]

Morality grounded in God explains our hunger for justice—our desire for a day of final reckoning when all wrongs are made right, when innocent suffering is finally redeemed, and when the guilty are punished and the righteous rewarded.

This also explains our own personal sense of dread. We feel guilty because we *are* guilty. We know deep down inside that we have offended a morally perfect being who has the legitimate authority to punish us. We also know we will have to answer for our own crimes against God.

Do you see why relativism is so attractive? Relativists seem to think if they can get rid of both morality and God, then guilt and judgment will disappear as well. It's like saying if we can eliminate doctors and hospitals, then disease and suffering will disappear, too. This is foolish.

In the end, we must accept one of two alternatives. Either relativism is true or morality is true. Either we live in a universe in which morality is a meaningless concept and thus we are forever condemned to silence regarding any moral issue, or moral rules exist and we're beholden to a moral God who holds us accountable to his law.

There are no other choices. As Francis Schaeffer put it, "These are not probability answers; [these] are the only answers. It is this or nothing."[5] If one is certainly false, the other is certainly true.

Notes

Introduction: Who Are You to Judge?

1. See Allan Bloom, *The Closing of the American Mind* (New York: Simon and Schuster, 1987), as well as James F. Harris, *Against Relativism* (Chicago: Open Court, 1992).

Chapter 1: The Death of Truth

1. Allan Bloom, *The Closing of the American Mind* (New York: Simon and Schuster, 1987), 25.

2. When Chuck Colson gave an address at Harvard titled "Why It's Impossible to Teach Ethics at Harvard Business School," this was precisely the response he received. As mentioned in a radio interview with James Dobson, Focus on the Family. The tape aired by Focus on the Family is Chuck Colson, "The Problem of Ethics: Why Good People Do Bad Things," an address to the Harvard Business School; copyright 1991, Prison Fellowship, P.O. Box 17500, Washington, D.C. 20041.

3. Kelly Monroe, ed., *Finding God at Harvard* (Grand Rapids: Zondervan, 1996), 15.

4. Ibid., 17.

5. Recorded in *The Presbyterian Layman*, July-August 1996, 8.

6. As told to Gregory Koukl by Jennifer Personius, November 1988.

7. *Los Angeles Times*, 22 August 1992, E4.

8. Dennis Prager, "Multiculturalism and the War Against Western Values" (audiotape), 7 October 1991, available through Ultimate Issues, 800-225-8584.

9. Stephanie Saul, *New York Newsday*, 20 July 1995, A17.

10. Ingrid Newkirk, national director of People for the Ethical Treatment of Animals (PETA), quoted in "To Market, To Market," *L.A. Times Magazine*, 22 March 1992.

11. *New York Times*, 26 March 1992 and 29 March 1992; *Time*, 6 April 1992; referenced in *World News Digest*, 13 April 1992.

12. Dennis Prager, "Just Another Two Days in the Decline of America," *The Prager Perspective*, 1 January 1997, 1.

13. C. S. Lewis, *The Abolition of Man* (New York: Collier Macmillan, 1955), 35.

Chapter 2: What Is Moral Relativism?

1. John Stuart Mill, *Utilitarianism* (Indianapolis: Bobbs-Merrill, 1957 [1861]), 61. Quoted in Hadley Arkes, *First Things* (Princeton: Princeton University Press, 1986), 25.

2. Gregory Koukl is speaking.

3. Relativists sometimes will attempt to universalize a personal moral principle by commending consistency. For example, if people determine that an act is wrong for them in one situation, it is wrong the next time they face that same situation. But this depends on the virtue of consistency, which itself depends on an absolute: One ought to be consistent.

4. Some people believe Albert Einstein proved that everything is relative. This, however, is false. Einstein's theories of relativity deal with a number of things, including the problems of absolute simultaneity and the idea of absolute motion. Both theories of relativity (general and special) depend, in part, on something nonrelative. They are based on a fixed constant, the speed of light. Neither theory has any ramifications for the question of morality.

5. See Tom L. Beauchamp, *Philosophical Ethics: An Introduction to Moral Philosophy* (New York: McGraw-Hill, 1991), 16–19.

6. David Hume, "Universal Principle of the Closed Frame," *The Enquiry Concerning Morals.*

7. Faye Wattleton holds a master's degree in maternal and infant care from Columbia University.

8. The Freedom of Access to Clinic Entrances Act (FACE). Passed in the Senate on 12 May 1994.

9. Kelly Monroe, ed., *Finding God at Harvard* (Grand Rapids: Zondervan, 1996), 18.

Chapter 3: Three Kinds of Relativism

1. This example is taken from Karl Duncker, "Ethical Relativity," *Mind* 48 (1939): 39–56. Duncker extracts it from *Voyage for the Discovery of a North-West Passage.* Quoted in Tom L. Beauchamp, *Philosophical Ethics: An Introduction to Moral Philosophy* (New York: McGraw-Hill, 1991), 39.

2. Beauchamp, *Philosophical Ethics*, 50.

3. Romans 14:2, 5, New American Standard Bible (NASB).

4. Judges 17:6 (NASB).

Chapter 4: Culture as Morality

1. William Graham Sumner, *Folkways* (Chicago: Ginn and Company, 1906), in *Ethical Theory: Classical and Contemporary Readings*, ed. Louis B. Pojman, (Belmont, Calif.: Wadsworth, 1995), 28.

2. Ibid., 22.

3. A trenchant critique of cultural relativism can be found in chap. 7 of Hadley Arkes, *First Things* (Princeton: Princeton University Press, 1986).

4. Tom L. Beauchamp, *Philosophical Ethics: An Introduction to Moral Philosophy* (New York: McGraw-Hill, 1991), 39.

5. Francis Beckwith uses this illustration in *Politically Correct Death* (Grand Rapids: Baker, 1993), 22.

6. C. S. Lewis, *Mere Christianity* (New York: Collier Macmillan, 1960), 5.

7. Sumner, *Folkways*, in *Ethical Theory*, ed. Pojman, 27.

8. Lillian Quigley, *The Blind Men and the Elephant* (New York: Charles Scribner's, 1959). Possible original sources of the story are the *Jataka Tales*, a collection of Buddhist birth stories, and the *Pancatantra Stories*, Hindu religious instruction fables.

9. Ibid.

10. Some have observed that values and morals have changed over time, which seems to imply that they are relative. This is simply a variation of Society Does Relativism from a different angle—not cultural, but temporal. The same deficiencies apply.

Chapter 5: Culture Defining Morality

1. This view is often inaccurately referred to as cultural relativism.

2. Louis P. Pojman, *Ethics: Discovering Right and Wrong* (Belmont, Calif.: Wadsworth, 1990), 23.

3. Ibid., 24.

4. John Warwick Montgomery, *The Law above the Law* (Minneapolis: Bethany House, 1975), 24.

5. Robert H. Jackson, "Closing Address in the Nuremberg Trial," in *Proceedings in the Trial of the Major War Criminals before the International Military Tribunal* (1948), quoted in Montgomery, *The Law above the Law*, 26.

6. Pojman, *Ethics*, 25.

Chapter 6: Moral Common Sense

1. Paul Edwards, ed., *The Encyclopedia of Philosophy*, vol. 4 (New York: Macmillan, 1967), 204.

2. St. Thomas Aquinas, *Summa Theologica* (London: Benzinger Brothers, 1911), Ia., Q84, a2, quoted in Louis P. Pojman, *What Can We Know? An Introduction to a Theory of Knowledge* (Belmont, Calif.: Wadsworth, 1995), 89.

3. Pojman, *What Can We Know?* 196.

4. C. S. Lewis, *The Abolition of Man* (New York: Macmillan, 1955), 53.

5. Aristotle, *Metaphysics*, 1006a.

6. Incidentally, this knife cuts both ways. When asked, "How do you know that?" one can respond with, "Why do you ask the question?" When the skeptic responds with, "Because you can't claim something is true unless you have proper justification," ask, "Oh? Well, how do you know *that?*" This reverses the process, putting the questioner on the slope slipping into infinity.

Chapter 7: Relativism's Seven Fatal Flaws

1. C. S. Lewis, *Mere Christianity* (New York: Macmillan, 1960), 31.

2. Even the phrase "if God is good . . ." used in the objection raises questions. Where did we get the idea of goodness, such that it would be good for God to get rid of evil? This way of thinking assumes that both objective good and objective evil exist.

3. Os Guinness, "The Journey: A Thinker's Guide to an Intelligent Faith," from an audiotaped presentation at the 1995 University of Michigan Veritas Forum. Available at 800-585-1070.

4. Lewis, *Mere Christianity*, 6–7.

5. Ibid., 5.

6. A. J. Ayer, "Emotivism," quoted in Louis P. Pojman, ed., *Ethical Theory: Classical and Contemporary Readings* (Belmont, Calif.: Wadsworth, 1995), 416.

7. Ibid.

8. Lewis, *Mere Christianity*, 3, 4.

9. The author here is Gregory Koukl.

10. I owe this insight to William Lane Craig.

11. The statement "There is no truth, therefore we ought to be tolerant to one another" actually asserts two truths, one rational and one moral: the first truth, that there is no truth, and the second, a moral truth that one ought to tolerate other people's viewpoints. The statement is contradictory on at least two counts.

12. J. P. Moreland, *Scaling the Secular City* (Grand Rapids: Baker: 1987), 247.

Chapter 8: Values Clarification

1. Allan Bloom, *The Closing of the American Mind* (New York: Simon and Schuster, 1987), 25.

2. William J. Bennett, "Revolt Against God: America's Spiritual Despair," *Policy Review* (winter 1994): 20.

3. Ibid. These statistics are documented in William J. Bennett, *The Index of Leading Cultural Indicators* (Washington, D.C.: The Heritage Foundation, 1993).

4. Sidney B. Simon, Leland W. Howe, and Howard Kirschenbaum, *Values Clarification*, rev. ed. (New York: Hart, 1978), back cover, 18–22. Quoted in Paul Vitz, "Why Values Clarification Must Be Rejected," in *Do the Right Thing: A Philosophical Dialogue on the Moral and Social Issues of Our Time*, ed. Francis J. Beckwith (Belmont, Calif.: Wadsworth, 1996), 83.

5. Vitz, "Why Values Clarification Must Be Rejected," 85.

6. The author here is Gregory Koukl.

7. Christina Hoff Sommers, "Teaching the Virtues," reprinted in *AFA Journal*, January 1992, 15.

8. Chuck Colson voiced the same objection when he wrote "Why It's Impossible to Teach Ethics at Harvard Business School." Because Harvard is relativistic, its business "ethics" simply collapse into pragmatism. If you cheat in business and get caught, you'll go to jail. The lesson? Either don't cheat, or don't get caught. Power matters, not morality. Might makes right.

9. Vitz, "Why Values Clarification Must Be Rejected," 86–87.

Chapter 9: Relativism's Offspring: Political Correctness and Multiculturalism

1. For an overview of the PC debate from different sides, see Francis J. Beckwith and Michael Bauman, eds., *Are You Politically Correct? Debating America's Cultural Standards* (Buffalo: Prometheus, 1993). See also Francis J. Beckwith, "The Epistemology of Political Correctness," *Public Affairs Quarterly* 8 (October 1994): 331–40.

2. Peter Kreeft and Ronald K. Tacelli, *Handbook of Christian Apologetics* (Downers Grove, Ill.: InterVarsity Press, 1994), 363–64.

3. See, for example, Irving Howe, "The Value of the Canon," in *Are You Politically Correct?* eds. Beckwith and Bauman, 133–46.

4. See Steven Yates, "Multiculturalism and Epistemology," *Public Affairs Quarterly* 6 (1992): 435–56.

5. Quoted in Beckwith and Bauman, eds., *Are You Politically Correct?*, 79.

6. As quoted in Dinesh D'Souza, *Illiberal Education: The Politics of Race and Sex on Campus* (New York: Free Press, 1991), 157.

7. For a critical analysis of postmodernism, see Dennis McCallum, ed., *The Death of Truth: What's Wrong with Multiculturalism, the Rejection of Reason, and the New Postmodern Diversity* (Minneapolis: Bethany House, 1996).

8. J. P. Moreland, *Scaling the Secular City* (Grand Rapids: Baker, 1987), 92.

9. Jung Min Choi and John W. Murphy, *The Politics and Philosophy of Political Correctness* (Westport, Conn.: Praeger, 1992), 93, 94.

10. Betty Jean Craige, *Reconnection: Dualism to Holism in Literary Study* (Athens, Ga.: University of Georgia Press, 1988), 111, as quoted in Jerry L. Martin, "The University as Agent of Social Transformation," *Academic Questions* 6 (summer 1993): 59.

11. Choi and Murphy, *Political Correctness*, 94.

12. Allan Bloom, *The Closing of the American Mind* (New York: Simon and Schuster, 1987), 25.

13. Certainly there are and have been a number of philosophers and ethicists who deny that moral claims are knowledge claims, yet they may not be epistemological relativists about other matters. But if one is an epistemological relativist about knowledge in general and one believes that moral claims are either not knowledge claims or they are knowledge claims relative only to an interpretive community, one nevertheless denies that moral claims have objective ontological status. (For more on these metaethical issues, see Moreland, *Scaling the Secular City*, 105–32.) It seems to us that those who defend the PC position are arguing that moral claims are knowledge claims but they are relative to an interpretive community.

14. Stanley Fish, "There's No Such Thing as Free Speech and It's a Good Thing, Too," in *Are You Politically Correct?* eds. Beckwith and Bauman, 51.

15. See, for example, Mortimer Adler, *Ten Philosophical Mistakes* (New York: Macmillan, 1985), 108–44, 156–200; Hadley Arkes, *First Things: An Inquiry into the First Principles of Morals and Justice* (Princeton: Princeton University Press, 1986); Francis J. Beckwith, *Politically Correct Death: Answering the Arguments for Abortion Rights* (Grand Rapids: Baker, 1993), 19–28; Donald S. Miller, "Multicultural Education: The Counselor's Prime Directive?" (professional paper, Master of Science in Marriage and Family Counseling, Graduate College, University of Nevada, Las Vegas, 1993); Moreland, *Scaling the Secular City*, 105–32; and Yates, "Multiculturalism and Epistemology."

16. Martin Luther King Jr., "Letter from the Birmingham Jail," in *The Right Thing to Do: Basic Readings in Moral Philosophy*, ed. James Rachels (New York: McGraw-Hill, 1989), 236–53. See also James Q. Wilson, *The Moral Sense* (New York: Free Press, 1993).

17. Choi and Murphy, *Political Correctness*, 94.

18. Tom L. Beauchamp, *Philosophical Ethics: An Introduction to Moral Philosophy* (New York: McGraw-Hill, 1982), 42.

19. Choi and Murphy, *Political Correctness*, 101.

20. Ibid.

21. Ibid.

22. Ibid., 2.

Chapter 10: On the Road to Barbarism

1. Molefi Kete Asante, *Afrocentricity*, rev. ed. (Trenton, 1988), as quoted in Arthur M. Schlesinger Jr., *The Disuniting of America: Reflections on Multicultural Society* (New York: W. W. Norton, 1992), 65.

2. George Reisman, "The Racist Road to Barbarism," in *Do the Right Thing: A Philosophical Dialogue on the Moral and Social Issues of Our Time*, ed. Francis J. Beckwith (Belmont, Calif.: Wadsworth, 1996), 413–19.

3. Ibid., 418.

4. Dinesh D'Souza, *Illiberal Education: The Politics of Race and Sex on Campus* (New York: Free Press, 1991), 201–02.

5. From *The Defender* 1, no. 2 (May 1994): 10.

6. Ibid.

7. See the cases documented in D'Souza, *Illiberal Education.*

8. "Faculty Statement Regarding Intellectual Freedom, Tolerance, and Prohibited Harassment" (State University of New York at Buffalo, 1988), as quoted in D'Souza, *Illiberal Education,* 9.

9. As cited in D'Souza, *Illiberal Education,* 9.

10. Anna Quindlen, "All of These You Are," *New York Times* (30 June 1992), as quoted in Dinesh D'Souza, *The End of Racism: Principles for a Multicultural Society* (New York: Free Press, 1995), 405.

11. Spike Lee, "The Playboy Interview," *Playboy* (July 1991): 52; "The Spike Lee Interview," *Rolling Stone* (11–25 July 1991), as quoted in D'Souza, *The End of Racism,* 405.

12. Danyel Smith, "Harry Allen: Hip Hop's Intellectual Assassin," *San Francisco Weekly* (13 February 1991): 1, as quoted in D'Souza, *The End of Racism,* 405.

13. Coramae Richey Mann, "The Reality of a Racist Criminal Justice System," *Criminal Justice Research Bulletin* 3.5 (1987): 2, as quoted in D'Souza, *The End of Racism,* 405.

14. Paula S. Rothenberg, ed., *Racism and Sexism: An Integrated Study* (New York: St. Martin's Press, 1988), 6, as quoted in D'Souza, *The End of Racism,* 405.

15. Romans 5:20 (NASB).

16. Although we oppose most preferential treatment programs in both the private and public sectors, we do believe that Christians of good will can disagree on this issue. The reason I (Frank) have shared my story is to show what happens when power replaces morality as the way in which difficult social issues are resolved.

17. Beckwith's ordeal is documented in Lloyd Billingsly, "The Ugly Sound of Racial Discord," *Washington Times* (14 November 1996). Beckwith's case against preferential treatment has been published as a policy analysis monograph: Francis J. Beckwith, *That's No White Male, That's My Husband, or Affirmative Action and the Civil Rights Vision* (Reno, Nev.: Nevada Policy Research Institute, 1996).

Chapter 11: Relativism and the Law

1. See John Rawls, *Political Liberalism* (New York: Columbia University Press, 1993); and John Rawls, *A Theory of Justice* (Cambridge: Harvard University Press, 1971).

2. Rawls, *Political Liberalism,* 22–28. Rawls's two principles of justice are:

"a. Each person has an equal claim to a fully adequate scheme of basic rights and liberties, which scheme is compatible with the same scheme for all; and in this scheme the equal political liberties, and only those liberties, are to be guaranteed their fair value.

"b. Social and economic inequalities are to satisfy two conditions: first, they are to be attached to positions and offices open to all under conditions of fair equality of opportunity; and second, they are to be to the greatest benefit of the least advantaged members of society." In Rawls, *Political Liberalism,* 5–6.

3. Rawls probably would not agree with our depiction of his view, for he considers his theory of justice to be deontological and not utilitarian nor egoistic. He writes that his principles of justice, like Immanuel Kant's, are categorical imperatives. See Rawls, *Theory of Justice,* 253. Some scholars, however, such as Michael Sandel (*Liberalism and the Limits of Justice* [New York: Cambridge University Press, 1983]), J. P. Moreland (in "Rawls and the Kantian Interpretation," *Simon Greenleaf Review of Law and Religion* 8 [1988–89]),

and Keith Pavlischek (*John Courtney Muray and the Dilemma of Religious Toleration* [Kirksville, Mo.: Thomas Jefferson University Press, 1994], 208–12) have assessed Rawls's theory similarly to our view.

4. See Rawls, *Political Liberalism*, 195–211. There are those to Rawls's political right, such as secular libertarians, who espouse state "neutrality" when it comes to questions of "the good." For example, libertarian social philosopher Murray Rothbard writes: "[W]hile the behavior of plants and at least the lower animals is determined by their biological nature or perhaps by their 'instincts,' the nature of man is such that *each individual person must, in order to act, choose his own ends and employ his own means in order to attain them.* Possessing no automatic instincts, each man must learn about himself and the world, *use his mind to select values,* learn about cause and effect, and act purposively to maintain himself and advance his life. . . . Since each individual must think, learn, value, and choose his or her ends and means in order to survive and flourish, the right of self-ownership gives man the right to perform these vital activities without being hampered and restricted by coercive molestation" (emphasis added). In Murray N. Rothbard, *For a New Liberty: The Libertarian Manifesto*, rev. ed. (San Francisco: Fox and Wilkes, 1978), 28, 29.

5. Justices Sandra Day O'Connor, Anthony Kennedy, and David Souter in "Planned Parenthood v. Casey (1992)," in *The Abortion Controversy: A Reader*, eds. Louis P. Pojman and Francis J. Beckwith (Belmont, Calif.: Wadsworth, 1994), 54.

6. Hadley Arkes, "A Pride of Bootless Friends: Some Melancholy Reflections on the Current State of the Pro-Life Movement," in *Life and Learning IV: Proceedings of the Fourth University Faculty for Life Conference*, ed. Joseph Koterski (Washington, D.C.: University Faculty for Life, 1995), 19.

7. As quoted in Russell Hittinger, "A Crisis of Legitimacy," *First Things: A Monthly Journal of Religion and Public Life* 67 (November 1996): 26.

8. As quoted in Timothy Egan, "Federal Judge Says Ban on Suicide Aid Is Unconstitutional," *New York Times* (5 May 1994), A24.

9. Ronald Dworkin, "When Is It Right to Die?" *New York Times* (17 May 1994), A19.

10. Hittinger, "A Crisis of Legitimacy," 26.

11. There are numerous defenses for the distinction between passive and active euthanasia. Two very good defenses are: J. P. Moreland, "James Rachels and the Active Euthanasia Debate," in *Do the Right Thing: A Philosophical Dialogue on the Moral and Social Issues of Our Time*, ed. Francis J. Beckwith (Belmont, Calif.: Wadsworth, 1996); and T. D. Sullivan, "Active and Passive Euthanasia: An Important Distinction?" in *Social Ethics*, eds. T. Mappes and J. Zembaty (New York: McGraw-Hill, 1982). No doubt there may be borderline cases when the distinction between passive and active euthanasia is difficult to make. But the Second Circuit did not claim that. It argued that the distinction was completely illegitimate.

12. As quoted in Hittinger, "A Crisis of Legitimacy," 26.

13. Hittinger, "A Crisis of Legitimacy," 26.

14. Ibid. In his article, Hittinger cites other cases as well as showing how the courts have arrived at their present state. See also Robert H. Bork, "Our Judicial Oligarchy," *First Things: A Monthly Journal of Religion and Public Life* 67 (November 1996): 21–24; and Hadley Arkes, "A Culture Corrupted," *First Things: A Monthly Journal of Religion and Public Life* 67 (November 1996): 30–33.

15. *Romer v Evans*, 1996 WL 262293, *8 (U.S.).

16. *Romer v Evans*, 1996 WL 262293, *2 (U.S.).

17. As quoted in Hittinger, "A Crisis of Legitimacy," 27.

18. Arkes, "A Culture Corrupted," 31, 32.

19. Ibid., 31.

20. In his critique of John Rawls's political philosophy, Michael Sandel makes a similar point by arguing that Rawls's view of the person (which Sandel refers to as "the unencumbered self"), far from being the neutral view that Rawls claims, is anticommunitarian. See Sandel, *Liberalism and the Limits of Justice.* See also Sandel's popular treatment of how this view of the self has negatively affected American political discourse, *Democracy's Discontent* (Cambridge: Harvard University Press, 1996), as well as Mary Ann Glendon, *Rights Talk: The Impoverishment of Political Discourse* (New York: Free Press, 1991).

21. J. P. Moreland, "A Defense of the Substance Dualist View of the Soul," *Christian Perspectives on Being Human: A Multidisciplinary Approach to Integration,* eds. J. P. Moreland and David M. Ciocchi (Grand Rapids: Baker, 1993), 71.

22. Ibid., 61.

23. These views include mind-body physicalism and property dualism. For a fuller discussion and a defense for substance dualism, see Moreland, "A Defense of the Substance Dualist View of the Soul," 64–77.

24. For a defense of substance dualism as it pertains to the human personhood of the fetus, see J. P. Moreland and John Mitchell, "Is the Human Person a Substance or a Property-Thing?" *Ethics and Medicine* 11:3 (1995): 50–55.

Chapter 12: Relativism and the Meaning of Marriage

1. As quoted in Hadley Arkes, "Odd Couples: The Defense of Marriage Act Will Firm Up the Authority of the States to Reject Gay Marriage," *National Review* 48 (12 August 1996): 48.

2. From the transcript of the television show *Think Tank,* aired on May 10, 1996. This episode, moderated by Ben Wattenberg, featured four guests who discussed the issue of homosexual marriage: William Eskridge, Hadley Arkes, Torie Osborn, and Anita Blair.

3. Ibid.

4. See, for example, the following works: Hadley Arkes, "Questions of Principle, Not Predictions: A Reply to Macedo," *The Georgetown Law Journal* 84 (1995); Robert P. George and Gerard V. Bradley, "Marriage and the Liberal Imagination," *The Georgetown Law Journal* 84 (1995); Jeffrey Satinover, *Homosexuality and the Politics of Truth* (Grand Rapids: Baker, 1996); and David Orgon Coolidge, *Same-Sex Marriage?* (Wynnewood, Penn.: Crossroads, 1996).

5. Arkes, "Odd Couples," 49.

6. Homosexual philosopher Richard Mohr has put forth a similar argument in his essay "Gay Basics: Some Questions, Facts, and Values," in *Do the Right Thing: A Philosophical Dialogue on the Moral and Social Issues of Our Time,* ed. Francis J. Beckwith (Belmont, Calif.: Wadsworth, 1996), 524–26. See also Stephen Macedo, "Homosexuality and the Conservative Mind," *The Georgetown Law Journal* 84 (1995).

7. Arkes, "Odd Couples," 49, 60.

8. Arkes, "Questions of Principle," 323.

9. Mortimer Adler, *Ten Philosophical Mistakes* (New York: Macmillan, 1985), 127.

10. Ibid.

11. George and Bradley, "Marriage and the Liberal Imagination," 307.

12. Harry V. Jaffa, "Sodomy and the Dissolution of Free Society," in *Do the Right Thing,* ed. Beckwith, 531.

13. Joseph Raz, *The Morality of Freedom* (1986), 162, as quoted in George and Bradley, "Marriage and the Liberal Imagination," 320. We do not know Mr. Raz's opinion on same-sex marriage, but we do know that he does not agree with our moral assessment of homosexual behavior.

Chapter 13: Relativism and the Meaning of Life

1. Take for example the work of philosopher Louis Pojman, a defender of abortion rights who is also a strong critic of moral relativism: Louis P. Pojman, "Abortion: A Defense of the Personhood Argument," in *The Abortion Controversy: A Reader*, eds. Louis P. Pojman and Francis J. Beckwith (Belmont, Calif.: Wadsworth, 1994), 254–69; Louis P. Pojman, "The Case for Moral Objectivism" in *Do the Right Thing: A Philosophical Dialogue on the Moral and Social Issues of Our Time*, ed. Francis J. Beckwith (Belmont, Calif.: Wadsworth, 1996), 10–18.

2. Although vitally important, the question of what constitutes suffering as well as the question of pain management and how each relates to the moral and legal justification of physician-assisted suicide are outside the scope of this book. For an informative discussion on these questions as they relate to the legal and political debate, see Robert Spitzer, "The Case Against Active Euthanasia," in *Life and Learning IV: Proceedings of the Fourth University Faculty for Life Conference*, ed. Joseph Koterski (Washington, D.C.: University Faculty for Life, 1995), 80–97.

3. For example, Tom Beauchamp and James Childress write: "Although respecting autonomy is more important than biomedical ethics had appreciated until the last two decades, it is not the only principle and should not be overvalued when it conflicts with other values. . . . In many clinical circumstances the weight of respect for autonomy is minimal, while the weight of nonmaleficence or beneficence is maximal. Similarly in public policy, the demands of justice can outweigh the demands of respect for autonomy." In Tom Beauchamp and James Childress, *Principles of Biomedical Ethics*, 3d ed. (New York: Oxford University Press, 1989), 112.

4. See, for example, Spitzer, "The Case Against Active Euthanasia"; John J. Conley, "Libertarian Euthanasia," in *Life and Learning IV*, 73–79; Victor Rosenblum and Clark Forsythe, "The Right to Assisted Suicide: Protection of Autonomy or an Open Door to Social Killing?" in *Do the Right Thing*, 208–21; J. P. Moreland, "James Rachels and the Active Euthanasia Debate," in *Do the Right Thing*, 239–46; and Patricia Wesley, "Dying Safely: An Analysis of 'A Case of Individualized Decision Making' by Timothy E. Quill, M.D.," in *Do the Right Thing*, 251–61.

5. See, for example, Francis J. Beckwith, *Politically Correct Death: Answering the Arguments for Abortion Rights* (Grand Rapids: Baker, 1993); Pojman and Beckwith, eds., *The Abortion Controversy;* and Patrick Lee, *Abortion and Unborn Human Life* (Washington, D.C.: The Catholic University of America Press, 1996).

6. Justice Harry Blackmun, "Excerpts from Opinion in *Roe v. Wade*," in *The Problem of Abortion*, 2d ed., ed. Joel Feinberg (Belmont, Calif.: Wadsworth, 1984), 195.

7. For an overview of what *Roe v. Wade* legally permits, see Beckwith, *Politically Correct Death*, 29–37.

Chapter 14: Tactics to Refute Relativism

1. Gregory Koukl is speaking.

2. Relativists may be using the "rational ought" here discussed in chapter 2 (i.e., it's irrational to impose one's morality, rather than immoral). If that's what they have in mind,

there is no contradiction. But this is almost never what relativists mean when they say, "Who are you to say?" They don't think you're simply mistaken; they think you did something wrong.

3. Louis P. Pojman, *Ethics: Discovering Right and Wrong* (Belmont, Calif.: Wadsworth, 1990), 37.

4. Ibid., 29.

5. One might argue that, since there are no clear moral absolutes, one is compelled by reason (not morality) to tolerate other behavior. In that sense, the assertion that "one ought to be tolerant" is not contradictory. Intolerance is not immoral in that case; it's unreasonable and irrational. But when most relativists argue for tolerance in light of what they believe to be the absence of moral absolutes, intolerance is viewed as a moral wrong, not a rational one. The language of blame is obvious. The relativist believes the moralizer has not done something foolish or incoherent; he's done something morally offensive.

6. Quoted in Kelly Monroe, ed., *Finding God at Harvard* (Grand Rapids: Zondervan, 1996), 66.

Chapter 15: Monkey Morality

1. Robert Wright, *The Moral Animal—Why We Are the Way We Are: The New Science of Evolutionary Psychology* (New York: Pantheon, 1994), 23.

2. Ibid., 58.

3. Ibid., 59.

4. Ibid., 56.

5. Ibid., 88.

6. Ibid., 13.

7. Ibid., 377.

8. Ibid., 102.

9. Thomas Hobbes, *Leviathan,* 1651.

10. Hadley Arkes, *First Things* (Princeton: Princeton University Press, 1986), 149.

11. Wright, *The Moral Animal,* 212.

12. Michael Ruse, "Evolutionary Theory and Christian Ethics," in *The Darwinian Paradigm* (London: Routledge, 1989), 262, 268–69. Quoted in William Lane Craig, "The Indispensability of Theological Meta-Ethical Foundations for Morality" (unpublished paper), 3.

Chapter 16: Why Morality?

1. Some object to the term "moral law" because moral laws can be broken, while scientific laws are inviolable. We have two responses. First, it's not obvious that scientific laws can never be violated. Miracles entail the suspension of natural law, and miracles seem to at least be possible, if not actual, unless one arbitrarily asserts naturalism. Second, moral laws are different from natural laws precisely at this point. The nature of a moral law is that it can be disobeyed by creatures with moral free will. If it couldn't be disobeyed, it wouldn't qualify as a moral law.

2. Richard Taylor, *Ethics, Faith, and Reason* (Englewood Cliffs, N.J.: Prentice-Hall, 1985), 83–84.

3. Quoted in Philip Yancey, "The Other Great Commission," *Christianity Today,* 7 October 1996, 136.

4. For a critique of Eastern thought as well as New Age thinking, see chap. 6 of Francis J. Beckwith and Stephen Parrish, *See the Gods Fall: Four Rivals to Christianity* (Joplin, Mo.: College Press, 1997).

5. Francis Schaeffer, *He Is There and He Is Not Silent,* vol. 1 of *The Complete Works of Francis Schaeffer* (Wheaton, Ill.: Crossway, 1982), 303.

Index

Abolition of Man, The (Lewis), 45
abortion, 45, 109, 116, 129, 135–38
absolutes, 63–66
absolutism, moral, 28–29
academic discourse, 102–4
accountability, 54–55, 61–63
Acuna, Rudy, 102, 103–4
Adler, Mortimer, 125
affirmative action, 103
afterlife, 134–35
amorality, 30
anthropology, 36–37, 46
anti–intellectualism, 102–4
apartheid, 53, 62, 88
approval, social, 120
Aristotle, 31, 57, 127
Arkes, Hadley, 110, 114–15, 123, 124, 161
art, 23
Asante, Molefi Kete, 93
authority, 168
autonomy, absolute personal: bondage of, 132; counterintuitiveness of, 132–34; fairness and, 107; justice and, 108; legal decisions and, 109–10, 113, 114; neutrality and, 115–16; physician-assisted suicide and, 129–31; rationale for, 131–32; same-sex marriages and, 120; suffering and, 134–35
Ayer, A. J., 67

Baby Garcia, 21–22
Beauchamp, Tom, 37, 38, 89
Beckwith, Frankie, 102, 104
behavior, 149–50, 160–61
beliefs, 147
Bennett, William, 75
Beyond Freedom and Dignity (Skinner), 65
bigotry, 102–3
Blackmun, Harry, 137–38
blame, 54–55, 65
Blind Men and the Elephant, The (Quigley), 47
Blind Watchmaker, The (Dawkins), 157
Bloom, Allan, 19, 73–74, 87
Bonhoeffer, Dietrich, 52
Book of Virtues, The (Bennett), 11
Bradley, Gerard V., 126–27
Bridges of Madison County, The, 11
Buddha, 31

California Civil Rights Initiative (CCRI), 102–3
censorship, 12
cheating, 77, 174n. 8
Choi, Jung Min, 83–84, 85–86, 89
civil rights, 52
Clarke, Ramsey, 62
classics, Western, 92
Clinton, Bill, 118
Closing of the American Mind, The (Bloom), 19, 73, 87
Cohen v. San Bernardino Valley College, 97
Colson, Chuck, 171n. 2, 174n. 8
commands, 166, 167–68
communities, interpretive, 83–84, 85–86, 87
Compassion in Dying, 111
Compassion in Dying v. Washington, 110, 111
conscience, 161–62
consistency, 172n. 3
contradictions, 55, 69, 143–47
conventionalism, 37–38, 49–53
correction, 146
Craig, William Lane, 59
Craige, Betty Jean, 83–84
Cuomo, Mario, 136

Dahmer, Jeffrey, 153
Dawkins, Richard, 157
Declaration of Independence, 59
Defense of Marriage Act (DOMA), 118–19
desires, 124
dignity, human, 21–22
disagreement, 149, 152
discourse, moral, 54–55, 67–68
diversity, 81
dogmatism, 74, 86–87
Dolfman, Professor, 96
DOMA (Defense of Marriage Act), 118–19
Dworkin, Ronald, 110, 112

Eastern religions, 170
Einstein, Albert, 94, 172n. 4
emotivism, 67
empiricism, 55
Encyclopedia of Philosophy, 56
epistemology, 47, 55–57, 79–80
errors, 26–27
Eskridge, William, 119
Establishment Clause, 113
ethics: of pleasure, 20–22; of power, 52, 77, 88, 95–97, 174n. 8; subjective, 28. *See also* morality
ethnocentrism, 92–95
Eurocentrism, 92, 94
euthanasia, 111, 177n. 11. *See also* physician-assisted suicide
evil, 54–55, 63–65
evolution, 156–64
evolutionary psychology, 157

fairness, 54–55, 65–66, 107
Ferraro, Geraldine, 136
Fieger, Geoffrey, 130, 132, 134
Finding God at Harvard (Monroe), 20, 33
First Amendment, 87–88
Fish, Stanley, 85, 87–88, 90–91
Folkways (Sumner), 43
foundational concepts, 59
Fourteenth Amendment, 109–10, 111, 112–13, 117, 133
freedom, human. *See* autonomy, absolute personal
freedom of speech, 53, 87–88
free expression, 98–99

Gandhi, Mahatma, 30, 31
genocide, 51
George, Robert P., 126–27
God, 156, 168–69
Gore, Al, 135–36
granny dumping, 23
guilt: explanation for, 169, 170; meaninglessness of, 62, 66; sense of, 166, 168
Guinness, Os, 64

habeas corpus, 53
harassment, 97–98
Harlan, John Marshall, 112–13
heroes, moral, 30–31
Herrnstein-Smith, Barbara, 82
Hillgren, Sonja, 130
history, 101
Hitler, Adolf, 13, 44, 52, 64, 155, 158. *See also* Nazism
Hittinger, Russell, 111
Holocaust, 51, 52, 64
Homer, 82
homosexuality, 112–15
hot buttons, 147–49, 152
human dignity, 101
human nature, 125
human rights, 59, 62, 124–25
Hume, David, 29

improvement, moral, 52–53, 54–55, 66–67
incest, 121, 122
incivility, 99
inconsistency: in evolutionary psychology, 159; of relativism, 11, 13, 143, 147–49, 153
infinite regress, 57, 173n. 6
injustice, 63
innocence, 62
intellectual liberty, 98–99
intent, 161
intuition, 55, 56–60, 147–48, 153–54
I Say Relativism: defined 38–39; law and, 107, 113; same-sex marriage and, 120; tolerance and, 154; universal moral notions and, 54–55

Jackson, Robert H., 51
Jaffa, Harry V., 127
Jesus Christ, 30, 31
judgments, 93
justice, 54–55, 63, 65–66, 108–9, 176n. 2
justification, 44–45

Kennedy, Anthony, 112–13, 116–17
Kevorkian, Jack, 130–32, 134–35
Kevorkianism. *See* autonomy, absolute personal
Kierkegaard, Søren, 169
King, Martin Luther Jr., 31, 52, 89
knowing and knowledge, 47, 55–57, 79–80
Kreeft, Peter, 80

Landers, Ann, 22
language, 147
Law above the Law, The (Montgomery), 50
law of noncontradiction, 55
laws, 51–52
Lee, Spike, 100
legislation, 33
Lewis, C. S.: on inconsistencies, 25; on intuition, 57; on morality, 45, 65, 156; on the problem of evil, 63; on treaties, 66
Los Angeles riots, 24–25

love, 122, 158
lying, 62

Mann, Coramae Richey, 101
Manson, Charles, 153
Mapplethorpe, Robert, 23
Maraldo, Pamela, 33
Marrietta College, 97
marriage: alternative forms of, 121–22; intrinsic value of, 125–38; love in, 122; sexual purpose of, 122–25; as social convention, 125–26. *See also* same-sex marriages
materialism, 166
mathematics, 27–28, 58, 59
media, 12
medicine, 133
Mere Christianity (Lewis), 156
Merton, Thomas, 169
Mill, John Stuart, 26
mind, 125
Miner, Judge, 111
Monroe, Kelly, 20, 33
Montgomery, John Warwick, 50
Moral Animal—Why We Are the Way We Are: The New Science of Evolutionary Psychology, The (Wright), 157
moral disputes, 90–91
morality: as accidental, 167–68; of animals, 160–61; behavior and, 160–61; characteristics of, 29; conflicting views on, 46; cultural, 36–37; denial of, 161–62; discussions of, 67–68; evolution and, 156–60, 161–62; existence of, 165–66; God and, 156, 168–69, 170; illiteracy in, 33–35; as illusion, 167; imposition of, 25, 32, 144–46; options for, 155; oughtness of, 26–27, 29, 162–63, 166, 168–69; pleasure and, 21; power and, 52; transcendent, 159; universal nature of, 29. *See also* ethics
moral law, 180n. 1
Moreland, J. P., 82, 116
mores, 43
Moses, 31
motives, 161
multiculturalism, 81–82, 89, 92–95. *See also* relativism, epistemological; relativism, value
murder, 44
Murphy, John W., 83–84, 85–86, 89

naturalism, 117, 166
natural law, 89
natural selection, 157–58
Nazism, 50–51, 86. *See also* Hitler, Adolf
neo-Nazism, 86
neutrality: abortion and, 136–38; lack of, 31–33, 115–16, 117; libertarian view of, 177n. 4; physician-assisted suicide and, 110; Rawls's view of, 108–9; same-sex marriage and, 119; sexual politics and, 113; in values clarification, 76–78
Niemöller, Martin, 52
norms, community, 83–84
norms, moral, 86, 89–90
Nuremberg trial, 50–51

objectivity, 47–48, 80
obligation, 26–27, 29. *See also* morality, oughtness of

Operation Rescue (OR), 136–37
opinion, 20, 64
original sin, 101
Osborn, Torie, 119

pain management, 179n. 2
Passantino, Gretchen, 102, 104
patricide, 37, 44
Paul the apostle, 31
perspective, cultural, 82–83
physician-assisted suicide, 110–11, 129–31
Planned Parenthood, 32, 33
Planned Parenthood v. Casey, 109–10, 111, 115, 133
Plantinga, Alvin, 144
pleasure, 20–22
Plessy v. Ferguson, 113
pluralism, 47, 136
Pojman, Louis, 49, 52, 56, 151, 179n. 1
political correctness, 79–82, 83, 88, 93. *See also* relativism, epistemological; relativism, value
politics, 88, 90–91
polygamy, 114, 121, 126
pornography, 23
positivism, legal, 50
postmodernism, 82
power, ethic of, 52, 77, 88, 95–97, 174n. 8
Prager, Dennis, 23, 24, 147
pragmatism, 174n. 8
praise, 54–55, 65
preferences, 38–39
prescription, 162–63
Prime Directive, 37–38
pro-choice, 62, 135–36. *See also* abortion
promise, 62
punishment, 26–27, 62, 66

Quarrel, The, 64
quarrels, 67–68
Quigley, Lillian, 47
Quill v. Vacco, 111
Quindlen, Anna, 100

racism, 62, 92, 93–94, 95, 100
Racism and Sexism (Rothenberg), 101
Raths, Louis, 75, 76
Rawls, John, 107–8, 112, 178n. 20
Raz, Joseph, 127
reformer's dilemma, 52
Reinhardt, Stephen, 110
Reisman, George, 94–95
relativism, cultural: circularity in, 152; critique of, 43–48; defined, 36–37; multiculturalism and, 95; tolerance and, 154
relativism, descriptive. *See* relativism, cultural
relativism, epistemological: defined, 79–80; dogmatism of, 86–87; moral claims and, 87–88, 175n. 13; moral norms in, 86; self-refuting claims of, 82–83, 84–86
relativism, individual ethical: defined 38–39; law and, 107, 113; same-sex marriage and, 120; tolerance and, 154; universal moral notions and, 54–55
relativism, moral: deficiencies of, 30–31; defined, 12–13; institutionalization of, 24. *See also* relativism, value

relativism, normative ethical, 37–38, 49–53, 154
relativism, personal subjective. *See* relativism, individual ethical
relativism, value: freedom of speech and, 87–88; invalid argument of, 90–91; norms in, 89–90; political correctness and, 88; tolerance and, 89–90. *See also* relativism, moral
relativity, theory of, 172n. 4
respect, 149
right to die, 110
Roe v. Wade, 109, 135, 137–38
Romer v. Evans, 112, 114, 119
Rothbard, Murray, 177n. 4
Rothenberg, Paul, 101
Rothstein, Barbara, 110

same-sex marriages: counterintuitive results of, 121–22; debate over, 128; DOMA and, 118–19; neutrality and, 119–20; opponents of, 120–21; purpose of sexuality and, 123–24. *See also* marriage
Sandel, Michael, 178n. 20
Sanger, Margaret, 32
Schaeffer, Francis, 19–20, 69, 170
schools, public, 75
science, 166
"Self-Definition: Morality" (Wattleton), 32–33
self-evident truths, 59
self-interest, 21
sensations, 57–58
sexual egalitarianism, 113–14, 120
sexuality, 123–25
sexual norms, 22
Sidgwick, Henry, 59
Simon, Sidney, 75, 76
skepticism, 20, 87
Skinner, B. F., 65
slavery, 52, 88, 137, 138
social construction theory, 120
social Darwinism, 159–60
Society Does Relativism: circularity in, 152; critique of, 43–48; defined, 36–37; multiculturalism and, 95; tolerance and, 154
Society Says Relativism, 37–38, 49–53, 154
sociopaths, 31
solipsism, 87
Sommers, Christina Hoff, 77
Souljah, Sister, 100
speciesism, 122
speech codes, 97–99
standards, 63–66
State University of New York at Buffalo, 97
subjectivism, 28, 38–39, 54–55
substance dualism, 116
suffering, 134–35, 179n. 2
suicide, 132–34
Sumner, William Graham, 43–44, 46–47, 48
suttee, 44–45

Tacelli, Ron, 80
tastes, 27
Taylor, Richard, 168
ten Boom, Corrie, 52
Teresa, Mother, 13, 30, 158
Think Tank, 119
Thomas Aquinas, 56
tolerance: abortion and, 136–37; contradiction and, 68–69, 180n. 5; definitions of, 149–50;

intolerance and, 24; neutrality and, 31–33; PC's claim of, 89–90; relativism and, 154–55; social, 120
treaties, 66
truth: death of, 19–20; objective, 27–28, 79–80; relativity of, 73–74; subjective, 27, 28

University of Connecticut, 97–98
University of Pennsylvania, 96, 99–100, 101

values: in cultural relativism, 43–44; determination of, 151; differences in, 44–45; existence of, 166; imposition of, 76, 77
values clarification, 75–78
Vitz, Paul, 76, 77

Walden II (Skinner), 65
war crimes, 50–51
Warnock, G. J., 59
Wattleton, Faye, 32–33
Wilberforce, William, 52
Wright, Robert, 157–60, 161–62

Yates, Steven, 81

Francis J. Beckwith (Ph.D., Fordham) is associate professor of philosophy, culture, and law and W. Howard Hoffman Scholar at the Trinity Graduate School, Trinity International University (Deerfield, Ill.), California campus. He is the author of numerous books, including *See the Gods* (College Press), *The Abortion Controversy Twenty-Five Years after Roe v. Wade*, rev. ed. (Wadsworth), *Affirmative Action: Social Justice or Reverse Discrimination?* (Prometheus), and *Politically Correct Death: Answering the Arguments for Abortion Rights* (Baker). He has contributed to numerous scholarly journals, including *Journal of Social Philosophy, International Philosophical Quarterly, Public Affairs Quarterly,* and *Ethics and Medicine.* His website is: www.iclnet.org/pub/resources/text/beckwith/beckwith-home. html.

Gregory Koukl earned an M.A. in apologetics from Simon Greenleaf University. He is the founder and executive director of Stand to Reason, an organization committed to training Christian thinkers and sending them into the public square in defense of classical Christianity and classical Christian values. He hosts the *Stand to Reason* radio talk show, an open forum in which he and callers discuss and debate issues of ethics, values, and religion. The Stand to Reason website is: www.str.org.

Revelation

1 Can't accuse others of evil doing

can't complain about the problem of evil